**DO NOT REMOVE
CARDS FROM POCKET**

**ALLEN COUNTY PUBLIC LIBRARY
FORT WAYNE, INDIANA 46802**

You may return this book to any agency, branch,

or bookmobile of the Allen County Public Library.

DEMCO

The Irwin Guide to Risk and Reward

A Basic Resource for Finance Professionals and Their Clients

Arefaine G. Yohannes, PhD
The University of Michigan—Dearborn

IRWIN
Professional Publishing®
Chicago • London • Singapore

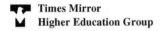

**Times Mirror
Higher Education Group**

Library of Congress Cataloging-in-Publication Data

Yohannes, A. (Arefaine)
   The Irwin guide to risk and reward / Arefaine G. Yohannes.
     p.   cm.
   Includes index.
   ISBN 0-7863-0704-8
    1. Investments. 2. Rate of return.   I. Title.
   HG4521.G15 1996
   658.15′54—dc20   95–44312

Printed in the United States of America
1 2 3 4 5 6 7 8 9 0 BS 3 2 1 0 9 8 7 6

About the Author

Arefaine G. Yohannes is an associate professor and chairman of the finance department at the University of Michigan, Dearborn. He holds a PhD degree in economics from Northwestern University. He has written computer programs for mortgages and has published a number of books and articles for various professional journals. He is also a registered investment advisor agent for H.D. Vest Advisory Services, Inc.

Preface

Two important considerations in making investments are return and risk. Returns consist of current incomes from investments and gains from the sales of investments or assets. Obviously, investors like to earn high returns from their investments. The problem is that investments with high returns often are associated with high risks. The higher the return, the higher the risk. To earn high returns, investors have to be willing to assume big risks.

Investors have to understand the risk–return relationship to make investment decisions that are appropriate for them. Conservative investors should select low-risk, low-return portfolios, and aggressive investors should select high-return, high-risk portfolios. In either case, investors should look for portfolios that promise the highest returns for any given levels of risk.

It is also important to understand the various measures of return and risk. That way investors can make appropriate comparisons of alternative investments. The problem is that it is difficult to find a single book that describes the various measures of return and risk. To understand the concepts and calculations of different types of returns, the interested investor would have to consult books, articles, and other publications on investments, insurance, real estate investments, real estate finance, or corporate finance.

The purpose of this book is to put together in one book the different measures of return and risk. The book covers the time value of money, general concepts of return, yields on bank accounts, Treasury bills, bonds, stocks, mutual funds, insurance, mortgages, business loans, and real estate investments. It also covers measures of portfolio performance, returns on capital expenditures, and measures of business profitability.

Measures of risk presented in this book include the standard deviation, the coefficient of variation, semivariance, beta, duration, convexity, liquidity, and debt ratios.

This book could be used as a supplement to regular textbooks in courses such as investments, real estate investments, and risk and insurance. It could also be a useful reference to financial professionals and investors.

The reader should not be discouraged by the number of formulas in the book. The formulas are easy to use. All the reader has to do is find the values of the variables in a formula, plug them into the formula, and perform the calculations. Numerical examples are used throughout the book to illustrate the uses of the formulas. Because some of the formulas use the summation sign, the summation sign is explained next.

THE SUMMATION SIGN

The summation sign (uppercase Greek sigma) is useful for *compactly* showing the sum of a series of values. A number of examples are used to show its uses. Consider the following data:

Year	Dividends per Share (D_i)
1	2
2	3
3	4

The sum of the annual dividends is as follows:

$$\sum_{i=1}^{3} D_i = D_1 + D_2 + D_3 = 2 + 3 + 4 = 9$$

The i at the bottom of the summation sign is called a *summation index*. The index value below the summation sign (=1) shows the starting value of the variable D, and the index value at the top of the summation sign (=3) shows the ending value of D. In this particular example, the values of D starting with the first and ending with the third are added together. If we want to add the second and the third values only, we would write the equation as follows:

$$\sum_{i=2}^{3} D_i = D_2 + D_3 = 3 + 4 = 7$$

If we want to add the first and the second values only, we would write the equation as follows:

$$\sum_{i=1}^{2} D_i = D_1 + D_2 = 2 + 3 = 5$$

If we want to square the first and the second values and add up the squared values, the equation would look like this:

$$\sum_{i=1}^{2} D_i^2 = D_1^2 + D_2^2 = 2^2 + 3^2 = 13$$

To show the multiplication of the sum by a constant, we write:

$$3 \times \sum_{i=1}^{2} D_i = 3(2 + 3) = 15$$

To show the division of the sum by a constant, we write:

$$\frac{\sum_{i=1}^{3} D_i}{3} = \frac{(2 + 3 + 4)}{3} = 3$$

To raise the sum to a power, such as square, we write:

$$\left(\sum_{i=1}^{2} D_i\right)^2 = (2 + 3)^2 = 25$$

Arefaine Yohannes

To Asmeret, Wubet, and Christine

Contents

Chapter One

Time Value of Money

A dollar today is worth more than a dollar a year from now, and a dollar a year from now is worth more than a dollar two years from now, and so on. The farther one goes into the future, the smaller the value of money will be. The time value of money refers to this declining value of money.

An alternative way of looking at the concept of the time value of money is to consider two extreme options. Suppose you are given a choice between $100,000 today and $100,000 forty years from now. You should choose $100,000 today. Only a fool would select $100,000 forty years from now. Although the dollar amounts are the same, they are not comparable because they relate to different points in time.

You can get a better perspective if you compare the $100,000 today with the present value of $100,000 forty years from now or if you compare $100,000 forty years from now with the future value of $100,000 today. If the interest rate is 10 percent per year, $100,000 today will grow to $4,525,925.56 forty years from now. Alternatively, $100,000 forty years from now is worth $2,209.49 today. When you compare $4,525,925.56 with $100,000 forty years from now or when you compare $2,209.49 with $100,000 today, the choice is clear. In the latter case, you can invest $100,000 today for forty years and have an accumulated value of more than $4.5 million.

In the previous paragraph, two concepts were introduced—future values and present values. These two concepts are essential for a full understanding of the time value of money.

THE FUTURE VALUE AND COMPOUNDING

A dollar invested today grows to a larger amount in the future if the interest rate is positive. As time goes by, the investment grows not only because of the interest earned on the original investment but also because of the interest earned on the interest. In other words, the investment grows because of the compounding effect.

The future value of the investment depends not only on the interest rate but also on the frequency of compounding and the period of the investment. The higher the interest rate, the greater the frequency of compounding; and the longer the time period, the larger the future value of the original investment tends to be.

Future Value of a Present Sum

The future value of a single sum today is calculated as follows:

$$FV_n = PV_0 [1 + (i/m)]^{mn}$$

where

FV_n = Future value in period n
PV_0 = Present value today
i = Annual interest rate
m = Frequency of compounding
n = Number of periods

Example.   A bank patron deposits $1,000 today. The bank pays 6 percent interest per year compounded annually. How much will the bank patron have five years from now? The answer is $1,338.23. This amount is determined as follows:

$$FV_n = 1,000 [1 + (0.06/1)]^{(1)5} = 1,338.23$$

If the bank pays 6 percent interest compounded monthly (12 times a year), the amount after five years would be $1,348.85.

Table 1–1 shows the effect of higher interest rates on the future value and Table 1–2 shows the effect of longer time on future values.

TABLE 1–1

	Present Value = $1,000 Time Horizon = 5 years			
Interest rate (%)	6	8	10	12
Future value ($)	1,338.23	1,469.33	1,610.51	1,762.34

TABLE 1–2

	Present Value = $1,000 Interest Rate = 6%			
Years	10	20	30	40
Future value ($)	1,790.85	3,207.14	5,743.49	10,285.72

Future Value Tables

There are financial tables that provide future value factors and other factors for simplifying calculations. Future value factors for single present amounts can be calculated using the following formula:

$$FVF_t = (1 + i)^t$$

where

FVF_t = Future value factor for period t
i = Periodic interest rate
t = Number of periods

Table 1–3 shows future value factors for three annual interest rates and five years.

Example. If the interest rate is 6 percent, the future value factor for year 5 would be 1.3382 and the future value of a current investment of $1,000 would be 1.3382 times 1,000, or $1,338.20.

TABLE 1–3
Future Value Factors for a Present Amount

		Interest Rates (%)	
Year	*6*	*8*	*10*
1	1.0600	1.0800	1.1000
2	1.1236	1.1664	1.2100
3	1.1910	1.2597	1.3310
4	1.2625	1.3605	1.4641
5	1.3382	1.4693	1.6105

Future Value of an Annuity

If the investor makes a series of equal investments or deposits at the end of each period, the future value of the investments would be calculated as follows:

$$FV_n = d \times \left[\frac{(1+i)^n - 1}{i} \right]$$

where

FV_n = Future value in period n
d = Periodic investments
i = Periodic interest rate
m = Number of periods in a year
n = Total number of periods

Example. A bank customer deposits $1,000 at the end of each year. The bank pays 6 percent interest per year compounded annually. At the end of five years, the customer will have $5,637.09, calculated as follows:

$$FV_5 = 1,000 \times \left[\frac{(1+0.06)^5 - 1}{0.06} \right] = 5,637.09$$

If the deposits are made at the end of each month and the bank pays 6 percent interest per year (0.5 percent per month) com-

TABLE 1–4

Years	Monthly Deposit ($) = 200 Annual Interest Rate = 10% Future Value ($)
10	40,969.00
20	151,873.77
30	452,097.58
40	1,264,815.91

pounded monthly, the amount after five years would be $69,770.03, calculated as follows:

$$FV_{60} = 1,000 \times \left[\frac{(1 + 0.005)^{5 \times 12} - 1}{0.005} \right] = 69,770.03$$

Table 1–4 shows the power of compounding when an investor invests $200 per month and earns 10 percent per year compounded monthly.

Future Value Factor for an Annuity

A table of future value factors for annuities can be constructed using the following formula:

$$FVF_t = \left[\frac{(1 + i)^t - 1}{i} \right]$$

where

FVF_t = Future value factor for period t

Table 1–5 shows future value factors for annuities for five years and three interest rates—6, 8, and 10 percent.

Example. If the interest rate is 6 percent, the future value factor for five years would be 5.6371 and the future value of $1,000 per year for five years would be 5.6371 times 1,000, or $5,637.10.

TABLE 1–5
Future Value Factors for Annuities

	Interest Rates (%)		
Year	6	8	10
1	1.0000	1.0000	1.0000
2	2.0600	2.0800	2.1000
3	3.1836	3.2464	3.3100
4	4.3746	4.5061	4.6410
5	5.6371	5.8666	6.1051

PRESENT VALUE OF A FUTURE AMOUNT

A dollar a year from now is worth less than a dollar today. A dollar two years from now is worth less than a dollar one year from now or a dollar today. In general the farther one goes into the future, the lower the present value of the dollar will be. The present value of a future dollar is determined through a process called *discounting* and discounting is the reverse of compounding.

Present Value of a Single Future Amount

The present value of a future amount depends on the interest rate and the time period. It is calculated as follows:

$$PV_0 = FV_n/(1 + i)^n$$

where

PV_0 = Present value
FV_n = Future value in period n
i = Periodic or annual interest rate
n = Number of periods or years

Example.   Suppose a friend promises to pay you $5,000 five years from now. If the interest rate is 6 percent per year, how much should you lend her today? In other words, what is the present value of the $5,000? The present value of $5,000 is $3,736.29. It is calculated as follows:

TABLE 1–6
Present Value Factors for a Future Amount

	Interest Rates (%)		
Year	*6*	*8*	*10*
1	0.9434	0.9259	0.9091
2	0.8900	0.8573	0.8264
3	0.8396	0.7938	0.7513
4	0.7921	0.7350	0.6830
5	0.7473	0.6806	0.6209

$PV_0 = 5,000/(1 + 0.06)5 = 3,736.29$

Present Value Factors for a Single Future Amount

Present value factors for single future amounts are determined using the following formula:

$PVF_t = [1/(1 + i)^t]$

where

PVF_t = Present value factor for period t

Table 1–6 shows present value or discount factors for five years and interest rates of 6, 8, and 10 percent.

Example. If the interest rate is 6 percent, the present value factor for year 5 would be 0.7473 and the present value of $5,000 five years from now would be 5,000 times 0.7473, or $3,736.5.

PRESENT VALUE OF AN ANNUITY

The present value of a series of equal payments at equal intervals in the future could be calculated as the sum of the present values of the individual payments. However, a more compact formula would be as follows:

$$PV_0 = P \times \left[\frac{1 - (1 + i)^{-n}}{i} \right]$$

where

PV_0 = Present value of the payments or cash flows
P = Periodic payment
i = Periodic interest rate or discount rate
n = Number of periods

Example. An investor is interested in buying a note that promises to pay $5,000 per year for four years. If the investor wants to earn 10 percent per year, how much should she pay for the note? In other words, what is the present value of the four annual cash inflows of $5,000? The answer is $15,849.33. It is calculated as follows:

$$PV_0 = 5,000 \times \left[\frac{1 - (1 + 0.10)^{-4}}{0.10} \right] = 15,849.33$$

Present Value Factors for Annuities

The present value factors for annuities are calculated using this formula:

$$PVF_t = \left[\frac{1 - (1 + i)^{-t}}{i} \right]$$

where

PVF_t = Present value factor in period t
i = Periodic interest rate or discount rate
t = Number of periods

Table 1–7 shows present value factors for annuities for interest rates of 6, 8, and 10 percent and five years.

Example. If the interest rate is 10 percent, the present value factor for year 4 would be 3.1699 and the present value of an annual cash flow of $5,000 for four years would be 5,000 times 3.1699, or $15,849.50.

TABLE 1–7
Present Value Factors for Annuities

Year	Interest Rates (%)		
	6	8	10
1	0.9434	0.9259	0.9091
2	1.8334	1.7833	1.7355
3	2.6730	2.5771	2.4869
4	3.4651	3.1321	3.1699
5	4.2124	3.9927	3.7908

Present Value of Uneven Cash Flows

In the previous section, the present value formula for annuities or even cash flows was presented. That formula is not appropriate for calculating the present value of a series of unequal cash flows. The present value formula for calculating a series of unequal cash flows is

$$PV_0 = P_0 + \frac{P_1}{(1+i)^1} + \frac{P_2}{(1+i)^2} + \ldots + \frac{P_n}{(1+i)^n}$$

where

P_0 = Payment or cash flow today or at period 0
PV_0 = Present value of the payments or cash flows
P_t = Payment or cash flow in period t
i = Periodic interest rate or discount rate
n = Number of periods

Example. Consider the following cash flows from a project:

Year	0	1	2	3
Cash flows	−10,000	4,000	4,500	5,000

Assuming an annual interest rate of 6 percent, the present value of these cash flows is $1,976.67, calculated as follows:

$$PV_0 = -10,000 + \frac{4,000}{(1 + 0.06)^1} + \frac{4,500}{(1 + 0.06)^2} + \frac{5,000}{(1 + 0.06)^3} = 1,976.67$$

SUGGESTED READINGS

Kaen, F. R. *Corporate Finance.* Cambridge, MA: Blackwell Publishers, 1995.

Kolb, R. W., and R. J. Rodriguez. *Principles of Finance.* Cambridge, MA: Blackwell Publishers, 1995.

Riggs, J. L., and T. M. West. *Engineering Economics.* New York: McGraw-Hill, 1986.

Van Horne, J. C. *Financial Management & Policy.* Englewood Cliffs, NJ: Prentice Hall, 1995.

Weston, J. F., and E. F. Brigham. *Managerial Finance.* Ft. Worth, TX: Dryden Press, 1992.

Chapter Two

Concepts and General Measures of Return

There are, essentially, two types of returns from investments. The first type of return is current income or income during the holding period of the asset. The second type of return is the gain from the sale of the asset. The total return of an investment includes the current income as well as the capital gain or loss.

PROMISED AND HISTORICAL RETURNS

The total return that an asset is expected to generate over a period of time is called the promised yield or return. It is also called an *ex-ante* return. On the other hand, the total return calculated from the actual or historical data is called the historical or *ex-post* return. Since investment decisions are based on the promised yield of an investment, the promised yield is normally positive. However, the historical or observed return could be positive or negative.

SINGLE-PERIOD RETURNS

The promised or historical return may be calculated for one period such as a year or for several periods (years). The total return for one period is calculated as follows:

$$TR = \frac{D + SP - PP}{PP}$$

where

TR = Total return
D = Average income per period
SP = Selling price of the asset
PP = Purchase price of the asset

Example.   An investor purchased a share of stock for $50 and sold it for $58 after one year. During the year, the investor received $2 in dividends. The historical total return realized for that year was

$$TR = \frac{2 + 58 - 50}{50} = 0.2$$

MULTIYEAR AVERAGE RETURNS

In calculating multiyear historical returns, an investor may use the annual arithmetic mean return or the annual geometric mean return.

Arithmetic Mean Return

The arithmetic mean return is, simply, the arithmetic average of the periodic returns. It is calculated as follows:

$$AMR = \frac{TR_1 + TR_2 + \ldots + TR_n}{n}$$

where

AMR = Arithmetic mean return
n = Holding period in years
TR_i = Total return in year i

The Geometric Mean Return

The geometric mean return is the compounded average rate of return over a specified period of time. There are three methods of calculating the geometric mean rate; these are discussed next.

Method 1.   Method 1 is used if the periodic returns are known. The formula for the geometric mean is

$$GMR = [(1 + TR_1)(1 + TR_2) \ldots (1 + TR_n)]^{1/n} - 1$$

where

GMR = Geometric mean return
TR_i = Total return in the ith year
n = Holding period in years

Example.

Year	1993	1994	1995	1996
Return (%)	6	8	9	10

$$AMR = (6\% + 8\% + 9\% + 10\%)/4 = 8.25\%$$

$$GMR = [(1 + .06)(1 + .08)(1 + .09)(1.1)]^{1/4} - 1 = 8.24\%$$

Method 2. The geometric mean return formula just presented is used when the periodic (annual) returns are available. If the periodic investment values are known rather than the periodic returns, the GMR is calculated as follows:

$$GMR = [(V_1/V_0)(V_2/V_1) \ldots (V_n/V_{n-1})]^{1/n} - 1$$

where

V_i = Investment value in the ith year
n = Holding period in years

Example. Consider the data in Table 2–1. The property value rose from \$100,000 in 1993 to \$126,247.70 in 1997. The geometric mean is 6 percent. It is calculated as follows:

$$GMR = [(106000/100000)(112360/106000)(119101.60/112360) \times$$
$$(126247.70/119101.6)]^{1/4} - 1$$

$$= 0.06$$

Method 3. If the periodic investment values are known, the method of least squares also may be used to compute the GMR from the following regression model:

$$V_t = a(1 + GMR)^t = ab^t$$

TABLE 2–1
Property Values

Year	Value
1993	$100,000.00
1994	106,000.00
1995	112,360.00
1996	119,101.60
1997	126,247.70

where

V	= Investment value
t	= Time (code numbers for periods)
a	= Parameter
b	= $(1 + GMR)$
GMR	= Geometric mean return

To estimate the GMR using the least squares method:

1. Linearize the regression model by taking the natural logs of both sides of the equation

$$ln\ V = ln\ a + t\ ln\ b$$

$$V' = a' + b't$$

where

V'	$= ln\ V$	= Natural log of V
a'	$= ln\ a$	= Natural log of a
b'	$= ln\ b$	= Natural log of b

2. Calculate b' and a'.

$$b' = \frac{n\sum tV' - \sum t \sum V'}{n\sum t^2 - \left(\sum t\right)^2}$$

$$a' = \frac{\sum V'}{n} - b'\frac{\sum t}{n}$$

TABLE 2–2

Year (t)	Property Value (V)	V' = ln V	t^2	$t \times V'$
0	$100,000.00	11.512925	0	0
1	106,000.00	11.571194	1	11.571194
2	112,360.00	11.629463	4	23.258926
3	119,101.60	11.687732	9	35.063196
4	126,247.70	11.746001	16	46.984004
10		58.147315	30	116.877320

where

n = Number of observations

3. Calculate the parameters of the original regression model and the *GMR*.

$$a = e^{a'}$$
$$b = e^{b'}$$
$$GMR = b - 1$$

Example. For a demonstration of this procedure, refer to Table 2–2.

$$b' = [5(116.877320) - 10(58.147315)]/[5(30) - 10^2] = 0.058269$$
$$a' = (58.147315/5) - 0.058269\,(10/5) = 11.512925$$
$$a = e^{11.512925} = 100,000$$
$$b = e^{0.058269} = 1.06$$
$$GMR = b - 1 = 1.06 - 1 = 0.06$$

This is the same result that was obtained earlier.

EXPECTED RETURN

Another measure of average return is the expected return. The expected return is the mean or average return in the probability sense and is appropriate for a situation of uncertainty. It is calculated as follows:

$$ER = p_1 \times TR_1 + p_2 \times TR_2 + \ldots + p_n \times TR_n$$

where

ER = Expected return
p_i = Probability of the ith return
TR_i = The ith possible return

Example.

Possible return (TR_i)	0.08	0.09	0.10
Probability of return (p_i)	0.20	0.50	0.30

Possible Return (1)	Probability of Return (2)	Weighted Possible Return (3) = (1)(2)
0.08	0.20	0.016
0.09	0.50	0.045
0.10	0.30	0.003
Expected Return =		0.064

NOMINAL VERSUS REAL RETURNS

The nominal return is the observed rate of return or interest rate whereas the real return is the inflation-adjusted return or interest rate. If the inflation rate is zero percent, there is no difference between the nominal return and the real return. In periods of inflation, however, the nominal return would be higher than the real return and the real return would be the more meaningful measure of return.

Given the nominal return and the inflation rate, the real return is calculated as follows:

$$i_R = \frac{i_N - r}{1 + r}$$

where

i_R = Real rate of return
i_N = Nominal rate of return
r = Inflation rate

Example. Suppose the nominal rate is 10 percent and the inflation rate is 5 percent. The real rate would be 4.76 percent, calculated as follows:

$$i_R = \frac{0.10 - 0.05}{1 + 0.05} = 0.0476$$

The real rate often is approximated by using only the numerator of the preceding formula. In other words, the approximate real rate is

$$i_R = i_N - r$$

For the prior example, the approximate real rate would be 5 percent (10% − 5%).

STRENGTHS AND WEAKNESSES

The arithmetic mean is very simple to calculate but not an accurate measure of the changes in wealth over time. Also it is not appropriate for situations of unertainty. The geometric mean return is more difficult to calculate than the arithmetic mean but it reflects changes in wealth more accurately over time. It is the correct measure for averaging ratios.

To see the difference between the arithmetic mean and the geometric mean, consider the following data:

Year	0	1	2
Investment value	1,000	2,000	1,000
Annual return		100%	−50%

Arithmetic mean return for the two-year period = 25%
Geometric mean return for the two-year period = 0%

The arithmetic mean return implies that the terminal value of the investment is higher than the initial value since the average return for the period was 25 percent. However, the terminal value is the same as the initial value. There was no growth. The geometric mean return reflects the absence of growth in the investment value. It is zero percent.

The expected return is appropriate for a situation of uncertainty. However, it is difficult to identify possible returns and their associated probabilities.

SUGGESTED READINGS

Francis, J. C. *Investments.* New York: McGraw-Hill, 1991.

Fuller, R. J., and J. L. Farrell, Jr. *Modern Investments & Security Analysis.* New York: McGraw-Hill, 1987.

Latane, H. A. "Criteria for Choice among Risky Ventures." *The Journal of Political Economy*, April 1959, pp. 144–55.

Mason, R. D. *Statistical Techniques in Business & Economics.* Burr Ridge, IL: Richard D. Irwin, 1983.

Young, W. E., and R. H. Trent. "Geometric Mean Approximations of Individual Security and Portfolio Performance." *Journal of Financial & Quantitative Analysis*, June 1969, pp. 179–99.

Chapter Three

The Annual Percentage Yield on Bank Deposits

There are various types of deposit accounts at depository institutions. They include interest-bearing checking accounts (negotiable order of withdrawal or NOW accounts, super-NOW acccounts, and share drafts), money market deposit accounts, passbook savings accounts, and certificates of deposit. The interest rate that depository institutions promise to pay on such deposits is called the *stated rate*. The stated rate may be fixed or variable (floating). In this chapter, we assume that the stated interest rate is fixed.

If the bank compounds interest more than once a year, the stated interest rate would understate the true interest rate on the deposit. The true interest rate is also called the *annual effective rate* or *annual percentage yield (APY)*; it is higher than the stated interest rate. The greater the frequency of compounding, the greater the amount by which the effective rate exceeds the stated rate.

CALCULATION OF THE ANNUAL PERCENTAGE YIELD

The APY can be calculated given either the interest rate or the interest amount.

APY When the Interest Rate Is Known

Given the stated interest rate and the frequency of compounding, the APY is calculated as follows:

$$APY = [1 + (i/m)]^m - 1$$

where

APY = Annual percentage yield
i   = Stated interest rate
m   = Frequency of compoundings per year

For continuous compounding (m = infinity), the APY would be:

$APY = e^i - 1$

where

e   = Base of the natural logarithmic or Naperian system =
            2.71828

   Example.   Suppose a bank promises to pay 5 percent interest compounded quarterly. The APY would be

$APY = [1 + (0.05/4)]^4 - 1 = 0.0509$ or 5.09%

If the bank compounds interest continuously, the APY would be

$APY = e^{0.05} - 1 = 0.051271$ or 5.1271%

For any given stated interest rate, the higher the frequency of compounding, the higher the APY to the bank customer. Table 3–1 shows the effect of the frequency of compounding on the APY for different levels of stated interest rates.

APY When the Interest Amount Is Known

When the dollar amount of the interest is known rather than the interest rate, the APY can be calculated as follows:

$APY = 100 \times [(1 + I/D)^{365/t} - 1]$

where

I   = Accrued interest
D   = Deposit amount
t   = Term of the deposit in days

For example, if the interest on a $5,000, 91-day certificate of deposit is $81.25, the APY, rounded to two decimal places, would be 6.68 percent.

TABLE 3–1
*Annual Percentage Yields for Different Stated Rates
and Compounding Frequencies*

	Selected Interest Rates (%)			
m	3	5	7	9
Annual	3.0000	5.0000	7.0000	9.0000
Semiannual	3.0225	5.0625	7.1225	9.2025
Quarterly	3.0339	5.0945	7.1859	9.3083
Monthly	3.0416	5.1162	7.2290	9.3807
Weekly	3.0446	5.1246	7.2458	9.4089
Daily	3.0453	5.1267	7.2501	9.4162
Continuous	3.0455	5.1271	7.2508	9.4174

m = Frequency of compounding

Annual Percentage Yield Earned (APYE)

For periodic statements on interest-bearing checking accounts, the depository institution has to calculate the APYE as follows:

$$APYE = 100 \times [(1 + I/ADB)^{365/t} - 1]$$

where

ADB = Average daily balance or average daily collected balance

The average daily balance will differ from the average daily collected balance if the depository institution does not start crediting interest the day the deposit is made. For example, if the institution credits interest the day after the deposit is made, the average daily collected balance will be smaller than the average daily balance but the difference will be small.

For example, if the interest on an average daily balance of $4,300 over a 30-day period is $11.61, the APYE would be 3.33 percent.

STRENGTHS AND WEAKNESSES

If banks and other depository institutions compound interest annually, the stated interest rate is equal to the APY and there is no need to distinguish between the two rates. However, if interest is compounded more than once a year, the APY is the appropriate measure of true yield and it exceeds the stated rate. The APY is fairly easy to calculate but the calculation assumes that the stated interest rate remains constant for the relevant period.

SUGGESTED READINGS

Financial Institutions Marketing Association. *Truth-in-Savings Marketing Compliance Guide—The Final Regulations.* Chicago: FIMA, 1992.

Morse, R. L. D. *Truth in Savings with Centsible Interest and Morse Rate Tables.* Manhattan, KS: Family Economics Trust Press, 1992.

Yohannes, A. G. *The Financial System and the Economy.* Minneapolis: Burgess International, 1990.

Chapter Four

Treasury Bill Returns

Treasury bills are short-term promisory notes issued by the United States Treasury. They are issued to finance budget deficits and to retire maturing liabilities. The minimum denomination is $10,000 and other denominations are sold in $5,000 increments. The Treasury bills mature in 3, 6, and 12 months. Newly issued Treasury bills are sold on an auction basis through the Federal Reserve Banks while previously issued bills can be purchased through securities brokers and banks.

The interest on a Treasury bill is called a *discount*. It is the difference between the price paid by the investor and the amount of money the Treasury promises to pay at maturity. For example, if an investor pays $9,800 for a six-month T-bill with a face value of $10,000, the interest or discount is $200 (10,000 – 9,800). The interest is paid by the Treasury at maturity as part of the face value of the T-bill. There are no interest payments between the time the investor buys the T-bill and maturity.

T-BILL DISCOUNT RATE

The ratio of the interest or discount to the face value of the T-bill is called the *discount rate*. The annualized T-bill discount rate is calculated as follows:

$$d = [(FV - P)/FV] \times (360/t)$$

where

d	=	Annual discount rate
FV	=	Face value of the T-bill
P	=	Price of the T-bill
t	=	Number of days to maturity

Example.   Suppose a $10,000, 90-day T-bill is sold for $9,900. The annualized discount rate is

$d = [(10,000 - 9,900)/10,000] \times (360/90) = 0.04$

The same result can be obtained by setting the face value at 100 and expressing the price as a percent of the face value. The calculation would be simpler since the face value and the price are smaller numbers. Also, the formula can be used for a T-bill with any denomination.

$d = [(100 - 99)/100] \times (360/90) = 0.04$

Given the discount rate, the discount and the price of the T-bill can be calculated as follows:

Discount $= d \times FV \times (t/360)$
Price $= FV - \text{Discount} = FV - [d \times FV \times (t/360)]$

For the previous example, the discount and the price of the T-bill are

Discount $= 0.04 \times 10,000 \times (90/360) = 100$
Price $= 10,000 - 100 = 9,900$

Asked Discount Rate and the Bid Discount Rate

Securities dealers in the secondary money markets buy and sell U.S. T-bills. Investors who wish to sell their T-bills before maturity can sell them to the securities dealers. Similarly, investors who wish to buy previously issued T-bills can buy the T-bills from the dealers. The price at which the dealer is willing to buy a T-bill from the investor is called the bid price and the price at which the dealer is willing to sell the T-bill to the investor is called the asked price. The asked price is larger than the bid price and the difference between the the two prices, the spread, represents income to the dealer.

The discount rate corresponding to the dealer's bid price is called the *bid discount rate* and the discount rate corresponding to the asked price is called the *asked discount rate*. You can use the previous formula to calculate both discount rates. If the bid price is used in the discount rate equation, you get the bid discount rate; if the asked price is used, you get the asked discount rate.

TABLE 4–1
Treasury Bills

Maturity	Days to Maturity	Bid	Asked	Change	Ask Yield
Oct. 10 '96	90	0.05	0.048	+0.01	0.0493
Feb. 13 '97	216	0.0525	0.052	–0.01	0.0542

The bid and the asked discount rates are reported in section 3 of *The Wall Street Journal* daily except weekends and holidays. Table 4–1 shows a hypothetical example.

The bid and asked prices can be calculated by solving the discount rate formula for the price. The price formula is

$$P = 100 - [100 \times d \times (t/360)]$$

where

d = Discount rate

Now, consider the Treasury bill with an October 10, 1996, maturity. The bid price is $98.75 per $100 of face value and the asked price is $98.80. They are calculated as follows:

Bid price $= 100 - [100 \times 0.05 \times (90/360)]$ $= 98.75$

Asked price $= 100 - [100 \times 0.048 \times (90/360)] = 98.80$

Although the discussion here focused on T-bills, the discount rate and yield formulas can be used to compute discount rates and yields of other short-term financial instruments such as commercial paper and bank acceptances.

Strengths and Weaknesses

Given the discount rate, it is fairly easy to calculate the discount and the price of the T-bill. However, the discount rate is not an adequate measure of yield on a T-bill investment for two reasons. First, the discount is divided by the face value. When calculating the yield, the discount should be divided by the price. Second, the discount rate formula uses a commercial year of 360 days to annualize the discount rate. To calculate the yield, the actual number of days in a year should be used.

TREASURY BILL BOND-EQUIVALENT YIELD

In the previous section of this chapter, it was pointed out that the discount rate is not an adequate measure of yield on a T-bill investment. A better measure of yield is the bond-equivalent yield. This measure is more accurate than the discount rate because:

- It is based on the actual number of days in a year, not 360 days.
- The discount is related to the price of the T-bill, not to the face value of the T-bill.

Calculation of the Bond-Equivalent Yield

For three-month and six-month T-bills, the bond-equivalent yield formula is

$$y = [(FV - P)/P] \times (365/t)$$

where

y = Annual bond-equivalent yield
FV = Face value of the T-bill
P = Price of the T-bill
t = Number of days to maturity

Example. Suppose a $10,000, 90-day T-bill is sold for $9,900. The bond-equivalent yield is

$$y = [(10,000 - 9,900)/9,900] \times (365/90) = 0.041, \text{ or } 4.1\%$$

The bond-equivalent yield also is reported in *The Wall Street Journal*. It is based on the asked price and is called the *asked yield*. In the section on discount rates, hypothetical T-bill quotes are shown.

TABLE 4–2
The Relationship between the Yield and Price

	FV	= $10,000	
	t (days to maturity) =	90	

Yield	4%	6%	8%
Price	9,902.33	9,854.21	9,806.56

For the T-bill with the October 10, 1996, maturity, the asked yield is 4.93 percent. This figure can be verified by using the bond-equivalent yield formula and the asked price of $98.80 calculated earlier. The asked yield is calculated as follows:

$$y = [(100 - 98.80)/98.80] \times (365/90) = 0.0493$$

Relationship between the Yield and the Price

If the bond-equivalent yield is known, the price of the T-bill can be calculated as follows:

$$P = (365 \times FV)/[(y \times t) + 365]$$

As you can see from the formula, there is an inverse relationship between the yield and the price. For a $10,000, 90-day T-bill, Table 4–2 shows the relationship between the yield and the price.

Relationship between the Discount Rate and the Yield

The discount rate and the bond-equivalent yield are related as follows:

$$y = (365 \times d)/[360 - (d \times t)]$$

As Table 4–3 shows, the bond-equivalent yield is always larger than the discount rate and the spread between the two rates widens with the increase in the discount rate and the increase in the maturity of the T-bill.

TABLE 4–3
The Relationship between the Discount Rate and the Yield

	Bond-Equivalent Yield	
Discount Rate	*t = 90 days*	*t = 180 days*
3%	3.06%	3.09%
6	6.18	6.27
9	9.34	9.56

Bond-Equivalent Yield for One-Year T-Bills

The calculation of the bond-equivalent yield for a one-year T-bill or any T-bill with a remaining term of more than six months to one year is much more involved than the calculation of a similar yield of a three-month or six-month T-bill. It is calculated as follows:

$$y = \frac{-B + \sqrt{B^2 - (4AC)}}{2A}$$

where

$A = [(t/2N) - 0.25]$
$B = t/N$
$C = (P - 100)/P$
$P =$ Purchase price per \$100 of face value
$t =$ Number of days to maturity
$N =$ Number of days in a year

Example. A T-bill with a remaining term of 275 days is sold for \$97.125 per \$100 of face value. The yield of this bond is 3.9 percent, calculated as follows:

$A = [\{275/(2 \times 365)\} - 0.25] = 0.126712329$
$B = t/N = 275/365 = 0.753424658$
$C = (P - 100)/P = (97.125 - 100)/97.125 = -0.02960103$
$y = 0.039,$ or 3.9%

Refer to the hypothetical T-bill quotes given earlier. The second T-bill matures on February 13, 1997. The number of days to maturity is 216 and the asked discount rate is 5.20 percent. Using the discount rate formula, the corresponding asked price of the T-bill is determined as follows:

Asked price = $100 - [100 \times 0.052 \times (216/360)] = 96.88$

Given the asked price of 96.88, the asked yield of 5.42 percent listed in the hypothetical example given earlier is calculated as follows:

$$A = [\{216/(2 \times 365)\} - 0.25] = 0.045890411$$
$$B = t/N = 216/365 = 0.591780822$$
$$C = (P - 100)/P = (96.88 - 100)/96.88 = -0.032204789$$
$$y = 0.0542, \text{ or } 5.42\%$$

Strengths and Weaknesses

For the reasons just stated, the bond-equivalent yield is a better measure of yield than the discount rate. However, the calculation of the price and the discount using the bond-equivalent yield is not as intuitive as it is with the discount rate. Furthermore, the calculation of the one-year T-bill yield is cumbersome.

SUGGESTED READINGS

Berlin, H. M. *The Dow Jones-Irwin Guide to Buying & Selling Treasury Securities.* Burr Ridge, IL: Dow Jones-Irwin, 1987.

Kish, R. J. "Discrepancy in Treasury Bill Yield Calculations." *Financial Practice & Education*, Spring/Summer 1992, pp. 41–45.

Kold, R. W. *Investments.* Cambridge, MA: Blackwell Publishers, 1995.

Rose, P. S. *Money & Capital Markets.* Burr Ridge, IL: Richard D. Irwin, 1994.

Stigum, M. *The Money Market.* Burr Ridge, IL: Richard D. Irwin, 1990.

_____. *Money Market Calculations.* Burr Ridge, IL: Dow Jones-Irwin, 1981.

Yohannes, A. G. *The Financial System & the Economy.* Minneapolis: Burgess International, 1990.

Chapter Five

Bond Yields

B onds are long-term promissory notes or debt instruments. They are issued by the federal government, state and local governments, and business corporations. Bonds issued by the federal government are called *Treasury bonds*; bonds issued by state and local governments are called *municipal bonds*; and bonds issued by business corporations are called *corporate bonds*. Bonds issued by quasi-government agencies are called *agency bonds*. Examples of such agencies are the Federal National Mortgage Association (Fannie Mae) and the Federal Home Loan Mortgage Corporation (Freddie Mac).

For coupon bonds, the issuer promises to pay interest semiannually and the face value at maturity. For zero-coupon bonds, the issuer promises to pay only the face value at maturity. There are no periodic interest payments. If the bond is callable, the issuer may call back the bond after the call-protection period ends by paying the call price.

The price at which the bond is sold may be higher than, equal to, or lower than the face value of the bond. If the price exceeds the face value, the bond is sold at a premium and the yield to maturity of the bond is lower than its coupon rate. If the face value is greater than the price of the bond, the bond is sold at a discount, and the yield to maturity is larger than the bond's coupon rate.

TYPES OF BOND YIELDS

There are five types of bond yields. They are the coupon rate (also called the *nominal yield*), the current yield, the effective yield, the yield to maturity, and the yield to call for callable bonds.

Coupon Rate

The coupon rate is the interest rate used to calculate the periodic interest payment on the bond. It is set at the time the bond is issued and remains the same until the bond matures or is called back. It is calculated as follows:

$CR = CP/FV$

where

CR = Coupon rate
CP = Annual coupon or interest payment
FV = Face value of the bond

 Example. Suppose the annual coupon payment is $60 and the face value is $1,000. The annual coupon rate would be

$CR = 60/1,000 = 0.06$, or 6%

Current Yield

The current yield is the ratio of the annual interest income to the current price of the bond. Unlike the coupon rate, the current yield varies with the price of the bond. Since it measures the interest income per dollar of investment in the bond, it is a better indicator of yield than the coupon rate.

The current yield (CY) is calculated as follows:

$CY = CP/PP$

where

CP = Coupon payment
PP = Current price of the bond

 Example. Suppose the annual interest payment is $60 and the current price is $990. The current yield would be

Current yield = $60/990 = 0.0606$, or 6.06%

In section 3, *The Wall Street Journal* reports the coupon rates and current yields of corporate bonds daily except weekends and holi-

TABLE 5–1
Corporate Bonds

Bonds	Cur Yld	Vol	Close	Net Chg
BBT 7 05	7.1	50	99	–1/8
MMG 8 15	8.2	70	99.5	+1/8

days. Hypothetical quotes are shown in Table 5–1. The first column shows the name of the company that issued the bond, the coupon rate, and the maturity year of the bond. The second column shows the current yield. The third column shows the number of bonds traded that day. The fourth column shows the the closing price of the bond.

For example, in the first row of Table 5–1, you see a BBT bond with a coupon rate of 7.0 percent maturing in 2005. For a face value of $1,000, the annual coupon payment would be $70 (= 0.07 × 1,000). The closing price is 99.0 percent of the $1,000 face value, or $990.00. The current yield of 7.1 percent listed in the second column is calculated by dividing 70 by 990.00.

Effective Yield

While the current yield is a better indicator of yield than the coupon rate, it is not an adequate measure of yield because it does not reflect capital gains or losses. The effective yield reflects not only the interest income from the bond but also any capital gains or losses.

In this section, we discuss the one-year effective yield and the multiyear approximate effective yield.

One-year effective yield.   The one-year yield measures the total return of a bond for one year. It is calculated as

$$OEY = \frac{CP + (P_1 - P_0)}{P_0}$$

where

OEY = One-year effective yield
CP = Coupon payment
P_0 = Price at the beginning of the year
P_1 = Price at the end of the year

Example. Consider the following bond data:

Interest paid last year   = $60
Price of the bond at the beginning of the year   =   980
Price of the bond at the end of the year   =   990

The one-year effective yield is 7.14 percent, calculated as

$$OEY = \frac{60 + (990 - 980)}{980} = 0.0714, \text{ or } 7.14\%$$

Multiyear approximate effective yield. The multiyear approximate effective yield also reflects interest income and any capital gains or losses. It is calculated as follows:

$$AEY = \frac{CP + \left[\dfrac{(SP - PP)}{n}\right]}{\dfrac{PP + SP}{2}}$$

where

AEY = Approximate effective yield
CP = Annual coupon payment
PP = Purchase price
SP = Selling price
n = Holding period in years

Example. Consider the following data:

Coupon payment $ 50
Purchase price   990
Selling price   1,010
Holding period in years   4

The approximate effective yield is 6.5 percent, calculated as follows:

$$AEY = \frac{60 + \left[\dfrac{(1{,}010 - 990)}{4}\right]}{\dfrac{990 + 1010}{2}} = 0.065, \text{ or } 6.5\%$$

Yield to Maturity

The yield to maturity is the yield that would result if the bond is held until maturity. The true yield to maturity takes into account all the cash flows of the bond as well as the time value of money. Since the calculation of this yield is complicated, a simpler but less accurate formula is used to approximate the true yield to maturity.

True yield to maturity. The true yield to maturity is calculated using the following equation:

$$PP = \frac{\dfrac{CP}{2}}{(1 + y)^1} + \frac{\dfrac{CP}{2}}{(1 + y)^2} + \ldots + \frac{\dfrac{CP}{2}}{(1 + y)^{2N}} + \frac{FV}{(1 + y)^{2N}}$$

where

y = Semiannual yield to maturity
N = Number of years to maturity
FV = Face value
PP = Purchase price
CP = Annual coupon payment

Example. Suppose an investor buys a 30-year bond for $990 today. The annual coupon payment is $60 paid semiannually and the face value is $1,000. What is the yield to maturity?

The yield to maturity is the value of y that equates the purchase price of the bond ($990) to the present value of the coupon payments and the face value (the right side of the following equation). It is calculated using a trial-and-error procedure.

$$990 = \frac{\dfrac{60}{2}}{(1+y)^1} + \frac{\dfrac{60}{2}}{(1+y)^2} + \ldots + \frac{\dfrac{60}{2}}{(1+y)^{2(30)}} + \frac{1{,}000}{(1+y)^{2(30)}}$$

Using a financial calculator, the semiannual yield to maturity (value of y) is determined to be 3.0364 percent and the annual yield to maturity is 6.0728 percent ($= 2 \times 3.0364\%$).

Approximate yield to maturity. The true yield to maturity can be approximated using the following simpler equation.

$$AYTM = \frac{CP + \left[\dfrac{(FV - PP)}{N}\right]}{\dfrac{PP + FV}{2}}$$

where

$AYTM =$ Approximate yield to maturity
$N \quad\ =$ Number of years to maturity
$FV \quad =$ Face value
$PP \quad =$ Purchase price
$CP \quad =$ Annual coupon payment

For the example in the previous section, the approximate yield to maturity is 6.06 percent, calculated as follows:

$$AYTM = \frac{60 + \left[\dfrac{(1{,}000 - 990)}{30}\right]}{\dfrac{990 + 1{,}000}{2}} = 0.0606, \text{ or } 6.06\%$$

Yield to Call

Some bonds are callable. This means the issuer can call back the bond before its maturity date. For example, if interest rates fall, the issuer may call back its bonds to issue new bonds with lower coupon rates. The issuer also may call back bonds to reduce or eliminate its debt.

There is usually a call-protection period during which the bond cannot be called back. After the call-protection period, however, the bond issuer can call back the bond at any time.

The yield to call is similar to the yield to maturity. However, it is calculated on the assumption that the bond will be held until the first call date. Obviously, there is no guarantee that the bond will ever be called or that it will be called on the first call date.

As with the yield to maturity, the true yield to call also can be approximated using a simpler formula.

True yield to call. The true yield to call is calculated on the assumption that the investor will receive interest payments until the first call date and the call price on the first call date. It is calculated using the following equation. The yield to call is the value of y that equates the two sides of the equation. It is calculated by trial and error.

$$PP = \frac{\frac{CP}{2}}{(1+y)^1} + \frac{\frac{CP}{2}}{(1+y)^2} + \ldots + \frac{\frac{CP}{2}}{(1+y)^{2nc}} + \frac{CAP}{(1+y)^{2nc}}$$

where

CAP = Call price
nc = Number of years to the first call date
y = Semiannual yield to call
PP = Purchase price of the bond
CP = Annual coupon payment

Example. Suppose an investor buys a 30-year callable bond for $990 today. The annual coupon payment is $60 payable semiannually and the company reserves the right to call back the bond anytime after five years. If the bond is called back at the end of the five-year period, the call price will be $1,060. What is the yield to call?

First, the appropriate values of the variables are plugged into the equation. Second, the value of y is determined by trial and error. For this example, a financial calculator is used to determine the true semiannual yield to call. It is determined to be 3.3767 percent and the annual yield to call is 6.7534 percent (2×3.3767 percent).

$$990 = \dfrac{\dfrac{60}{2}}{(1+y)^1} + \dfrac{\dfrac{60}{2}}{(1+y)^2} + \ldots + \dfrac{\dfrac{60}{2}}{(1+y)^{2(5)}} + \dfrac{1{,}060}{(1+y)^{2(5)}}$$

Approximate yield to call (AYTC). The yield to call can be approximated using a formula similar to the formula used to approximate the yield to maturity. The approximation formula is

$$AYTC = \dfrac{CP + \left[\dfrac{(CAP - PP)}{nc} \right]}{\dfrac{PP + CAP}{2}}$$

For the callable bond example in the previous section, the approximate yield to call is 7.22 percent. It is calculated as follows:

$$AYTC = \dfrac{60 + \left[\dfrac{(1{,}060 - 990)}{5} \right]}{\dfrac{990 + 1{,}060}{2}} = 0.0722, \text{ or } 7.22\%$$

The Wall Street Journal reports the coupon rates and yields to maturity of U.S. Treasury bonds and notes daily except weekends and holidays. Table 5–2 shows hypothetical quotes of Treasury notes and Treasury bonds. The first column shows the coupon rate or the nominal yield. The next column shows the maturity month and year. If there is an *n* next to the maturity year, the security is a Treasury note; if there is no *n*, it is a Treasury bond.

The next two columns show the bid and the asked prices respectively, where the bid price is the dealer's purchase price and the asked price is the dealer's selling price. The prices are expressed as percentages of par values. If the price is 100, the bond is selling at par, which means the market price of the bond is equal to the face value or maturity value of the bond. If the price is greater than 100, the bond is selling at a premium, which means the price is greater

TABLE 5–2
Treasury Bonds and Notes

Rate	Maturity Mo/Yr	Bid	Asked	Ask Yld.
8	May 11	100:26	100:28	7.9
8	August 12	99:28	100:00	8.0
8	May 16	101:21	101:24	7.8
8	August 13–18	95:26	95:28	8.5

than the face value. The premium is the difference between the price and the face value. Finally, if the price is less than 100, the bond is selling at a discount, which means the price is smaller than the face value. The discount is the difference between the face value and the price.

The asked yield is shown in the last column. This yield is the yield to maturity of the note or bond based on the asked price of the note or the bond. For callable bonds that are selling at premiums, the *Journal* reports the yields to the earliest call dates. For callable bonds that are selling at discounts, the asked yields are the yields to maturity. You can recognize a callable bond if there are two numbers separated by a hyphen. For example, the fourth bond is a callable bond. The coupon rate is 8 percent and the bond can be called any time between August 2013 and 2018. Since the asked price, 95:28, is smaller than 100, the asked yield is the yield to call and is equal to the yield to maturity.

The prices are quoted in 32nds. For example, 101:16 means the price is 101 and 16/32 percent of face value. For a face value of $1,000, the asked price is $1,015.00. Also note that when the price of the bond is equal to the face value, the yield is equal to the coupon rate. The second bond is an example of this.

Yield of a Zero-Coupon Bond

For bonds that do not pay periodic interest, the coupon rate and the current yield do not apply. The effective yield and the yield to maturity are calculated as follows:

Effective yield (EY) $= [(SP/PP)^{1/n} - 1]$

Yield to maturity $(YTM) = [(FV/PP)^{1/N} - 1]$

where

PP = Purchase price
SP = Selling price
FV = Face value
n = Holding period in years
N = Years to maturity

Example. Consider a 30-year, $1,000 zero-coupon bond with a current price of $250. Suppose the estimated selling price of the bond two years from now is $300. What is the effective yield? What is the yield to maturity?

Effective yield $= [(300/250)^{1/2} - 1] = 0.0954$

Yield to maturity $= [(1,000/250)^{1/30} - 1] = 0.0473$

Yields of Consols or Perpetual Bonds

Although rare, some bonds do not have maturity dates and therefore do not have maturity values. However, they pay periodic interest forever and they can be sold. Such bonds are called consols or perpetual bonds.

Clearly, the coupon rate and the yield to maturity do not apply. However, the current yield and the effective yield can be calculated using the formulas given earlier.

Yields of Bonds Sold between Interest Payment Dates

Normally, coupon bonds pay interest semiannually. If a bond is sold on an interest payment date, the effective yield, the yield to maturity, and the yield to call can be calculated using the preceding formulas. However, if a bond is sold between interest payment dates, different formulas would apply. The current value or price of the bond would be the present value of the expected cash flows (interest plus face value) minus the accrued interest.

For example, if a bond pays interest semiannually, and the next interest payment date is September 1, the value of the bond on May 1 would be the present value of the expected cash flows minus the interest for the months of March and April. The next interest payment would be received by the buyer of the bond, but since the seller is entitled to the interest income for the months of March and April, the accrued interest has to be subtracted from the present value of the future cash flows.

The yield of a bond sold between interest payment dates is calculated by solving for y in the following equation:

$$PP = \frac{PVNIPD}{(1+y)^{[180 - ((w \times 30) + k)]/180}} - \left[\frac{CP}{2} \times (((w \times 30) + k)/180) \right]$$

where

$$PVNIPD = \frac{\frac{CP}{2}}{(1+y)^1} + \frac{\frac{CP}{2}}{(1+y)^2} + \ldots + \frac{\frac{CP}{2}}{(1+y)^{2N}} + \frac{FV}{(1+y)^{2N}} + \frac{CP}{2}$$

PP = Current value of the bond

$PVNIPD$ = Present value of the cash flows of the bond as of the next interest payment date plus the next coupon payment

y = Semiannual yield

w = Number of whole months since the last interest payment date

30 = Number of days in a commercial month; used for corporate, municipal, and some agency bonds

k = Number of days since the first day of the current month

180 = Number of days in a commercial semiannual period; used for corporate, municipal, and some agency bonds

CP = Annual coupon payment

FV = Estimated future selling price of the bond when solving for the effective yield

= Face value when solving for the yield to maturity

$\qquad$ = Call price when solving for the yield to call

N $\qquad$ = Number of years to the sale date from the next interest payment date when calculating the effective yield

$\qquad$ = Number of years to maturity from the next interest payment date when calculating the yield to maturity

$\qquad$ = Number of years to the first call date when calculating the yield to call

Example. Consider a $1,000 bond with a semiannual coupon payment of $30. The price of this bond on May 5 was $966.61. The next interest payment date is September 1 and the bond will mature 1.5 years after the next interest payment date. What is the annual yield to maturity?

The last interest payment date was March 1. So, the number of whole months since that date is 2. Since the number of days from the beginning of the current month is 5, the total number of days since the last interest payment date is $(2 \times 30) + 5$, or 65.

The semiannual yield to maturity is the value of y in the price equation given in this section that equates the current value of the bond ($966.61) to the present value of the cash flows from the bond minus accrued interest (on the right side). The value of y is determined using the trial-and-error procedure.

At $y = 3.5$ percent, the value of the right side of the equation is $983.07. This amount is bigger than the current value of $966.61. We should try a higher value for y. At $y = 4.5$ percent, the right side value is $950.51. The value of y that we are looking for is between 3.5 percent and 4.5 percent. By interpolation, the desired value of y is found to be 4.0055283 percent. Thus, the annual yield to maturity is, approximately, 8.01 percent.

Tax-Exempt Yields and Taxable Corporate Yields

In general, municipal bonds, that is, bonds issued by state and local governments, are not subject to federal income taxes, but corporate bonds are. As a result, yields on municipal or tax-exempt bonds tend to be lower than yields on corporate bonds. The difference between the two yields is called the tax premium.

Given an investor's marginal tax rate, we can determine the yield on a corporate bond that is equivalent to a particular yield on a tax-exempt bond as follows:

$$CBY = \frac{TEBY}{[1 - (FTR + STR - (FTR \times STR))]}$$

where

CBY	=	Corporate bond yield
TEBY	=	Tax-exempt bond yield
FTR	=	Investor's federal marginal tax rate
STR	=	Investor's state marginal tax rate

Since the combined federal and state tax rate is the sum of the federal and state tax rates minus the product of the two tax rates, the previous equation can be written as

$$CBY = TEBY / (1 - CTR)$$

where

CTR= Combined federal and state tax rate

Example. Consider the following data:

Tax-exempt bond yield	7%
Federal marginal tax rate	31
State marginal tax rate	4

The equivalent yield on a corporate bond is 10.57 percent, calculated as follows:

$$CBY = 0.07 / [1 - \{0.31 + 0.04 - (0.31 \times 0.04)\}] = 0.1057$$

This equation is used to construct a matrix that shows the relationships between the taxable corporate bond yield, the tax-exempt yield, and the combined federal and state tax rate. For example, for an investor in the 28 percent federal tax bracket, a tax-exempt yield of 8 percent is equivalent to a taxable yield of 11.57 percent. See Table 5–3.

TABLE 5–3

Taxable Corporate Bond Yields for Different Tax-Exempt Yields and Marginal Tax Rates

Federal Marginal Tax Rate	Combined Tax Rate*	Tax-Exempt Yields (%)		
		6	8	10
15	18.40	7.35	9.80	12.26
28	30.88	8.68	11.57	14.47
31	33.76	9.06	12.08	15.08
36	38.56	9.77	13.02	16.28
39.6	42.02	10.35	13.80	17.25

* Assumes a state tax rate of 4 percent.

For simplicity, some people ignore state income tax rates and the yield equivalence formula is written as

$$CBY = TEBY/(1 - FTR)$$

where

$FTR =$ Investor's federal marginal tax rate

For an investor in the 28 percent tax rate, a tax-exempt yield of 8 percent is equivalent to a corporate bond yield of 11.11 percent. In a state where the income tax rate is 4 percent, the exact equivalent corporate bond yield would be 11.57 percent, 46 basis points (i.e., 0.46 percent) higher than the approximate equivalent corporate bond yield of 11.11 percent. Naturally, the higher the state and local income tax rates, the greater the inaccuracy. For example, if the state income tax rate is 6 percent and the tax-exempt yield is 8 percent, the exact equivalent corporate bond yield would be 11.82 percent and the approximate equivalent yield would be 11.11 percent, a difference of 71 basis points. Table 5–4 ignores state income tax rates.

Obviously, the approximation formula would yield a more exact result in states where there are no income taxes, such as Texas, Alaska, and Florida.

The Wall Street Journal reports the coupon rates and bid yields to maturity of active tax-exempt or municipal bonds in section 3.

TABLE 5–4
Taxable Corporate Bond Yields for Different Tax-Exempt Yields and Marginal Tax Rates

Federal Marginal Tax Rate	Tax-Exempt Yields (%)		
	6	8	10
15	7.06	9.41	11.76
28	8.33	11.11	13.89
31	8.70	11.59	14.49
36	9.38	12.50	15.63
39.6	9.93	13.24	16.56

STRENGTHS AND WEAKNESSES

A number of bond yield measures were discussed in this chapter. The coupon rate or the nominal yield is useful for calculating the annual or semiannual interest payment but it is not a good measure of return because it ignores capital gains and losses and is applied not to the price of the bond but to the face value.

The current yield is a better measure of return than the coupon rate because it is related to the current price of the bond, but like the coupon rate, it ignores capital gains or losses.

The effective yield, the yield to maturity and the yield to call could take into account the time value of money, interest, and capital gains or losses. However, without financial calculators or computers, the calculations are cumbersome because they require the use of the trial-and-error procedure. The approximation formulas simplify the calculations of those yields but at a loss of some accuracy. The approximation formulas ignore the time value of money.

SUGGESTED REFERENCES

Berlin, H. *The Dow Jones-Irwin Guide to Buying & Selling Treasury Securities.* Burr Ridge, IL: Dow Jones-Irwin, 1987.

Fabozzi, F. J. *Fixed Income Mathematics.* Chicago: Probus Publishing, 1988.

Francis, J. C. *Management of Investments*. New York: McGraw-Hill, 1993.

Reilly, F. K., and E. A. Norton. *Investments*. Ft. Worth, TX: Dryden Press, 1995.

Rose, P. S. *Money and Capital Markets*. Burr Ridge, IL: Richard D. Irwin, 1994.

Yohannes, A. G. *The Financial System & the Economy*. Minneapolis: Burgess International, 1990.

Stock Returns

Investors buy stocks for dividend income, price appreciation, or both. For example, people who need current income would tend to invest in stocks that pay high current dividend income while investors who do not need current income until a much later time would tend to invest in stocks that offer the potential for large price appreciation. Many stocks pay dividends and still offer capital gains.

TYPES OF YIELDS

There are basically two measures of stock yield—the dividend yield and the effective yield. The effective yield may be calculated for a single period like one year or for several periods or years.

Dividend Yield

The dividend yield is the ratio of the annual dividends paid to the current price of the stock. It is similar to a bond's current yield. For example, if the annual dividend paid by a company is $4 and the current price of the stock is $40, the dividend yield would be 10 percent. Since the dividend yield does not take into account capital gains or losses on a stock investment, it is not an adequate measure of stock yield.

The Wall Street Journal reports dividend yields of hundreds of corporations. Table 6–1 shows hypothetical stock quotes. For the first company on the list, BBT, the amount of dividends per share was $0.50 and the closing price (close) of the stock was $20.00. The reported dividend yield of 2.5 percent is calculated by dividing 0.50 by 20.00.

TABLE 6–1
Hypothetical Stock Quotes

| 52 Weeks | | | | | | | Vol | | | | Net |
Hi	Lo	Stock	Sym	Div	Yld (%)	PE	100s	Hi	Lo	Close	Chg.
22	12	BBT	BBT	0.50	2.5	10	200	20	19.5	20	+1/8
52	32	MMG	MMG	1.35	3.00	15	400	48	48	48	—

In Table 6–1, the first two columns show the highest and lowest prices of the stock in the last 52-week period. The third and fourth columns show the name of the company that issued the stock and the stock symbol. The fifth and sixth columns show the amount of dividends per share and the dividend yield. The seventh and eighth columns show the price-earnings ratio and the number of shares traded that day. The following three columns show the highest, lowest, and the closing prices of the stock that day. The last column shows the change in the closing price relative to the closing price the day before.

One-Year Effective Yield

The effective yield overcomes the drawback of the dividend yield. It takes into account the two components of return from a stock investment—dividends and capital gains or losses.

The effective yield for one period is measured as follows:

$$EY = [D + (P_1 - P_0)]/P_0$$

where

EY = Effective yield
D = Dividend paid
P_0 = Price at the beginning of the period
P_1 = Price at the end of the period

Example. Consider the following stock data:

Dividends paid last year   = $ 4
Price of the stock at the beginning of the year =   50
Price of the stock at the end of the year   =   56

The one-year effective yield is 20 percent, calculated as

$$EY = [4 + (56 - 50)]/50 = 0.20$$

Annualizing monthly or quarterly yields. If monthly or quarterly data are available, the one-period yield formula can be used to calculate the monthly or quarterly yield. The compounded annual yield may then be calculated from the monthly or quarterly yields by adding one to each yield, multiplying the adjusted yields together, and subtracting one from the result.

For example, if the quarterly yields calculated by using the formula in the previous section are 5, 6, 7, and 8 percent, the compounded annual yield would be

$$y = [(1 + .05)(1 + .06)(1 + .07)(1 + .08)] - 1 = 0.2862, \text{ or } 28.62\%$$

The One-Year Effective Yield on a Margin Investment

An investor can open a cash account or a margin account at a stock brokerage house. In a cash account, the investor uses his or her own cash to make an investment. In a margin account, the investor can borrow a portion of the price of the stock from the broker to buy stocks. The current initial margin (Regulation T margin) for stock investments is 50 percent. This means the minimum down payment on a stock investment is 50 percent and the maximum amount that the investor can borrow from the broker is 50 percent of the price of the stock.

If the price of the stock increases, the loan increases the investor's return on equity. On the other hand, if the price of the stock decreases, the loan magnifies the investor's losses.

The one-year effective yield on a margin investment is calculated as follows:

$$EYM = [D + (P_1 - P_0) - i (1 - m)P_0]/m \times P_0$$

where

EYM = Effective yield on a margin investment
D = Dividends paid
P_0 = Price of the stock at the beginning of the year
P_1 = Price of the stock at the end of the year
i = Annual interest rate on the margin loan
m = Initial margin in percent

Example. Consider the following data on a margin investment:

Price of the stock at the beginning of the year	=	$50
Price of the stock at the end of the year	=	56
Dividends paid last year	=	4
Annual interest rate on the margin loan	=	8%
Initial margin	=	50%

The one-year yield on this investment is 32 percent, calculated as

$$EYM = [4 + (56 - 50) - 0.08\,(1 - 0.50)\,50]/(0.50 \text{ ö } 50) = 0.32, \text{ or } 32\%$$

Note that this return of 32 percent is higher than the 20 percent return on the unleveraged investment in the previous section.

Multiyear Effective Yield

Once the one-year yields are determined, the multiyear effective yield can be determined. The multiyear effective yield is the compounded average annual return on a stock investment. It is the same as the geometric mean return and is calculated as follows:

$$MEY = [(1 + y_1)(1 + y_2) \dots (1 + y_n)]^{1/n} - 1$$

where

MEY = Multiyear effective yield
y_i = Historical effective yield in year i
n = Holding period in years

Example. Consider the following historical data:

Year	1	2	3	4
Effective yield	6%	8%	4%	15%

The compounded average annual effective yield or geometric mean return for the four-year period is 8.17 percent, calculated as follows:

$$MEY = [(1+0.06)(1+0.08)(1+0.04)(1+0.15)]^{1/4} - 1$$
$$= 0.0817, \text{or } 8.17\%$$

Approximate Annual Effective Yield

If the average annual dividend income (D), the purchase price (PP), the selling price of the stock (SP), and the holding period (n) are known, the average annual effective yield can be approximated as follows:

$$y = \frac{D + \dfrac{SP - PP}{n}}{\dfrac{PP + SP}{2}}$$

Example. Consider the following stock data:

Average annual dividends	=	$ 4
Purchase price of the stock	=	50
Selling price of the stock	=	56
Holding period in years	=	3

The approximate average annual effective yield is 11.32 percent, calculated as follows:

$$y = \frac{4 + \dfrac{56 - 50}{3}}{\dfrac{50 + 56}{2}} = 0.1132$$

STRENGTHS AND WEAKNESSES

Essentially, there are two measures of stock yields—the dividend yield and the effective yield. The dividend yield is based on dividend income only and ignores the other major component of stock return—the capital gain or loss. The effective yield includes both dividends and capital gains or losses.

SUGGESTED READINGS

Francis, J. C. *The Management of Investments*. New York: McGraw-Hill, 1993.

Gitman, L. J., and M. D. Joehnk. *Fundamentals of Investing*. New York: Harper-Collins, 1993.

Kolb, R. W. *Investments*. Cambridge, MA: Blackwell Publishers, 1995.

Radcliffe, R. C. *Investment*. New York: Harper-Collins, 1994.

Yohannes, A. G. *The Financial System & the Economy*. Minneapolis: Burgess International, 1990.

Chapter Seven

Mutual Fund Returns

Mutual funds are institutions that invest in a variety of investment products. They may be classified on the basis of their investment objectives or the types of products in which they invest. On the basis of investment objectives, mutual funds may be grouped broadly into growth funds if capital appreciation is their primary objective and income funds if their primary objective is current income.

On the basis of the products in which they invest, mutual funds may be classified into stock funds, bond funds, money market funds, tax-exempt funds, government funds, international funds, or sector funds.

Mutual funds offer immediate diversification, professional money management, economies of scale, and low initial and subsequent minimum investment requirements. In addition to these general advantages, they pay dividends and make capital gains distributions. They also offer the potential for capital appreciation.

A number of measures of return are used in the mutual fund industry. For money market mutual funds, there are the seven-day yield and the seven-day effective yield. For mutual funds, the measures of return include the cumulative total return, the average annual total return, the distribution rate, the Securities and Exchange Commission (SEC) yield, and the Dietz algorithm.

TYPES OF YIELDS

Seven-Day Money Market Yield

The money market yield is calculated for a seven-day period and then annualized. Based on a hypothetical account having one share, it is calculated as follows:

$$y = \frac{V_7 - V_0 - E}{V_0} \times \frac{365}{7}$$

where

y = Seven-day yield
V_0 = Value of one share at the beginning of the seven-day period
V_7 = Value of the share at the end of the seven-day period
E = Expenses

Example. Consider the following data:

Share value at the beginning of the seven-day period = $1.00
Share value at the end of the seven-day period   =   1.001
Expenses per share   =   0.0001

The seven-day yield is 4.69 percent, calculated as follows:

$y = [(1.001 - 1.00 - 0.0001)/1.0] \times (365/7) = 0.0469$, or 4.69%

Seven-Day Money Market Effective Yield

The effective yield is the compounded annual yield based on the seven-day return. It is calculated as follows:

$$EY = \left[1 + \frac{V_7 - V_0 - E}{V_0}\right]^{365/7} - 1$$

For the example in the previous section, the effective yield is

$EY = [1 + 0.0009]^{365/7} - 1 = 1.048 - 1 = 0.048$, or 4.8%

Note that the effective yield exceeds the yield because the effective yield reflects the effects of compounding.

Mutual Fund Dividend Yield

The dividend yield is the ratio of the annualized dividends (including interest) to the maximum offering price of a share on the last payble date for load funds. For B shares or for no-load funds, the denominator is the net asset value on the last payable date. The dividends are annualized by multiplying the monthly dividends by 12. For municipal bond funds, dividends are annualized by calculating the daily dividend rate and then multiplying it by 365.

For example, if the last month's dividend and interest payment of a mutual fund is $0.10 , and the offering price is $20, the dividend yield would be 6 percent, calculated as follows:

$$DY = (MD \times 12)/OP = (0.10 \times 12)/ 20 = 0.06, \text{ or } 6\%$$

where

MD = Dividends and interest for the last month
OP = Offering price

Distribution Rate or Yield

The distribution yield or rate is similar to the dividend yield except that it includes capital gains distributions. It is calculated as

$$DR = (D \times 12)/OP$$

where

DR = Annualized distribution rate
D = Distribution of dividends and capital gains for the last month
OP = Maximum offering price on the payable date

Here again, for no-load funds or for B shares, the net asset value is used in lieu of the offering price. For municipal bond funds, the daily distribution rate is first calculated and then annualized by multiplying it by 365. For example, if the one-month distribution of dividends and capital gains is $0.12 and offering price is $20, the distribution yield would be 7.2 percent.

SEC Yield

If a mutual fund advertises its yield, it is required to furnish what the industry calls the *Securities and Exchange Commission standardized yield*. The SEC yield is an annualized bond-equivalent yield based on the net investment income per share. It is calculated using this formula:

$$Y = 2\left[\left(\frac{a-b}{cd}+1\right)^6 - 1\right]$$

where

Y = SEC yield
a = Dividends and interest earned for the most recent 30-day period
b = Expenses for the period
c = Average daily number of shares outstanding
d = Maximum offering price per share on the last day of the period

Example. Consider the following data:

30-day dividend and interest income	=	$70,000
30-day expenses	=	$7,500
Average daily number of shares outstanding	=	1,000,000
Maximum offering price on the last day of the period	=	$10

The SEC yield is 7.62 percent, calculated as

$$Y = 2\left[\left(\frac{70,000 - 7,500}{1,000,000 \times 10}+1\right)^6 - 1\right] = 0.0762$$

Mutual Fund Cumulative Total Return

The cumulative total return refers to the change in the value of a mutual fund investment over a period of time assuming that dividends and capital gains distributions are invested. It is calculated as follows:

$$CTR = [(EV/BV) - 1] \times 100$$

where

CTR = Cumulative total return
EV = Ending value
BV = Beginning value = Initial gross investment

Example.   Consider the following data:

Initial gross investment   = $10,000
Value after 10 years = Ending value = $50,000
Sales load   =   4.5%

The cumulative total return on the gross investment, including the 4.5 percent sales load, is 400 percent. This return also is called the load-adjusted CTR and is calculated as follows:

$$CTR = [50,000/10,000) - 1] \times 100 = 400.00\%$$

The net investment is $10,000 \times (1 - 0.045) = \$9,550$ and the cumulative total return on the net investment is

$$CTR = [50,000/9,550) - 1] \times 100 = 423.56\%$$

Note that if you have the beginning value and ending value for just one year, the CTR would be the total return for the year.

Average Annual Total Return

The average annual total return is a hypothetical compounded average annual return at which the initial investment grows to the ending value over a period of time. It is calculated as follows:

$$ATR = [(EV/BV)^{1/n} - 1] \times 100$$

where

ATR = Annual total return
EV = Terminal value
BV = Beginning value
n = Holding period

Example.   Consider the following data:

Initial investment   = $10,000
Value after 10 years = Ending value = $50,000
Sales load   =   4.5%

The ATR on the gross investment (i.e., the load-adjusted ATR) is

$ATR = [(50,000/10,000)^{1/10} - 1] \times 100 = 17.46\%$

The ATR on the net investment is 18 percent, calculated as follows:

$ATR = [\{50,000/(10,000 \times (1 - 0.045))\}^{1/10} - 1] \times 100 = 0.18$, or 18%

If the ending and beginning values are not available, the ATR may be calculated from the CTR.

$ATR = [(100 + CTR)/100]^{1/n} - 1$

For example, if the CTR is 400 percent and the holding period is 10 years, the ATR would be

$ATR = [\{(100 + 400)/100\}^{1/10} - 1] \times 100 = 17.46\%$

Total Return When Dividends and Capital Gains Are Distributed

In the previous sections, the calculations assumed that dividends and capital gains were reinvested. If the dividends and capital gains are distributed, the total return is calculated as follows:

$TR = [(EV - BV + D)/BV] \times 100$

where

D   = Distributions of dividends and capital gains

Example.   Consider the following data:

Beginning value	=	$1,000
Ending value after one year	=	1,100
Dividends and capital gains distributions	=	100

The total return for the year is 20 percent, calculated as

$TR = [(1,100 - 1,000 + 100)/1,000] \times 100 = 20\%$

This formula assumes that there were no new investments or withdrawals during the year. If the investor makes additional investments or redeems shares, the Dietz algorithm may be used.

Dietz Algorithm

If you make additional investments or liquidate some shares, you can use the Dietz algorithm to calculate the total return on your mutual fund investment. The Dietz algorithm formula is

$$TR = \left[\frac{EV - (0.5 \times NA)}{BV + (0.5 \times NA)} - 1 \right] \times 100$$

where

EV = Ending value
BV = Beginning value
NA = Net additions = Additional investments – Withdrawals

Example. Consider the following mutual fund data:

Value at the beginning of the year	=	$10,000
Value at the end of the year	=	13,500
Investment at the end of the first quarter	=	2,500
Withdrawal at the end of the second quarter	=	1,500
Distributions	=	400

The net addition during the year is $2,500 – 1,500 = $1,000 and the total return is 23.81 percent, calculated as follows:

$$TR = \left[\frac{13,500 - (0.5 \times 1000)}{10,000 + (0.5 \times 1000)} - 1 \right] \times 100 = 23.81\%$$

If there are dividend and capital gain distributions, the numerator has to be adjusted as follows:

$$TR = \left[\frac{EV - (0.5 \times NA) + D}{BV + (0.5 \times NA)} - 1 \right] \times 100$$

where

EV = Ending value
BV = Beginning value
NA = Net additions = Additional investments – Withdrawals
D = Distributions of dividends and capital gains

Using the preceding data, the TR would be 27.62 percent, calculated as follows:

$$TR = \left[\frac{13,500 - (0.5 \times 1,000) + 400}{10,000 + (0.5 \times 1,000)} - 1 \right] \times 100 = 27.62\%$$

The Dietz algorithm assumes that the investments and withdrawals occur in the middle of the year. This assumption is better than ignoring additions and withdrawals of capital but it does lack some accuracy because it assumes that the net contributions occur at midyear. Accuracy can be improved by applying the formula on a monthly or a quarterly basis and linking the monthly or quarterly returns to get an annual total return. Although it could mean considerable work, the return also can be calculated every time there is an investment or a withdrawal. The returns then can be linked to get an annual total return. The annual return is obtained by adding one to each return, multiplying the returns together, and then subtracting one.

The Wall Street Journal reports mutual fund statistics including total return data in section 3. Specifically, the *Journal* reports the fund name, the fund's investment objective, the net asset value, the offer price, the change in the net asset value, and total return data for different periods.

SUGGESTED READINGS

Dorf, R. C. *The New Mutual Fund Investment Advisor.* Chicago: Probus Publishing, 1986.

Frailey, F. "How to Tell How You Are Doing." *Changing Times*, January 1988, pp. 37–42.

Markese, John. "How Has Your Portfolio Done? Calculating Your Return." *AAII Journal*, September 1990, pp. 28–32.

Securities and Exchange Commission. *Investment Company Registration Package.* Washington, DC, 1993.

Stark, Ellen. "How You Do as an Investor." *Money*, December 1993, p. 146.

Chapter Eight

Measures of Portfolio Performance

We examined measures of yields on individual stocks, bonds, and other instruments in earlier chapters. In this chapter, we present alternative measures of portfolio returns.

A portfolio is a group of investment assets. It may include stocks, bonds, money market securities, and real assets. The portfolio may consist of individual stocks, individual bonds, mutual funds shares, or a combination of a variety of investment assets.

Portfolio returns show how much money investors are making or losing. They also show the money management skills of money managers. To show the relative performance of portfolios, the portfolio returns are compared to returns on broad stock or bond indexes.

MEASURES OF PORTFOLIO PERFORMANCE

There are several measures of portfolio performance. They include the time-weighted return, the original and modified Dietz algorithms, the original and modified Bank Administration Institute (BAI) returns, and risk-adjusted measures of return. The risk-adjusted measures are the reward-to-variability ratio (the Sharpe measure) and the reward-to-volatility ratio (the Treynor measure).

Cumulative Time-Weighted Return

The basic measure of return of a portfolio is calculated by subtracting the beginning value from the ending value and dividing the difference by the beginning value. If incomes were distributed during the period and the distributions were not reinvested, the distributed incomes are added to the difference between the ending and beginning values and then divided by the beginning values.

However, this basic measure of return is inadequate if there are additions to and withdrawals from the portfolio during the measurement period. In a situation like this, the time-weighted return is the appropriate measure of return.

The calculation of the time-weighted return requires:

1. The determination of the market value of the portfolio on the day of the addition or withdrawal.
2. Calculation of the return between cash flow points using the basic measure of return.
3. Linking the returns between the cash flow points to get the cumulative return for the relevant period.

   Example.   Consider the following data:

Date	Market Value before Addition or Withdrawal	Addition or Withdrawl	Market Value after Addition or Withdrawal
4/01/95	$5,000		$5,000
5/01/95	5,500	$ –500	5,000
6/15/95	4,800	1,200	6,000
6/30/95	6,360	0	6,360

$$TWR = [(5500/5000)(4800/5000)(6360/6000) - 1] \times 100$$
$$= [1.1 \times 0.96 \times 1.06] - 1$$
$$= 11.94\%$$

The time-weighted return is the most appropriate return when there are cash inflows and outflows between the beginning and ending values. However, there are two problems with this approach. First, it is not always possible to get market prices on the dates of the cash flows. Second, if the frequency of additions and withdrawals is high, the determination of market values and the computation of the time-weighted return can be burdensome. For these reasons other measures may have to be used.

Original Dietz Algorithm

The Dietz algorithm assumes that the net additions (additions less withdrawals) are made at the midpoint of the return measurement period. The return then is calculated as follows:

$$r = \left[\frac{EV - 0.5(NA) + I}{BV + 0.5(NA)} - 1 \right] \times 100$$

where

r = Portfolio return
EV = Ending value
NA = Net additions = Additions – Withdrawals
I = Income distributed during the period
BV = Beginning value

For the example in the previous section, the Dietz algorithm yields a return of 12.34 percent. First, the net addition is determined by subtracting the withdrawals from the additions. It is $700 (1,200 – 500). Second, the return is calculated as follows:

$$r = \left[\frac{6{,}360 - 0.5(700) + 0}{5{,}000 + 0.5(700)} - 1 \right] \times 100 = 0.1234 = 12.34\%$$

The Dietz algorithm is easy to use and it does not require the valuation of a portfolio each time an investment or liquidation of shares occurs. However, it does not recognize the exact timing of cash flows and with irregular cash flows, it tends to be less reliable.

Modified Dietz Algorithm

The modified Dietz algorithm improves on the original Dietz algorithm by explicitly recognizing the timing of cash flows. The modified Dietz formula is

$$r = \left[\frac{EV - BV - NA + I}{BV + WF} - 1 \right] \times 100$$

where

r = Return
EV = Ending value
NA = Net additions = Additions – Withdrawals
I = Income distributed during the period
BV = Beginning value
WF = Weighted cash flows (additions or withdrawals)

The weighted cash flows (additions or withdrawals between the beginning and ending values) are calculated as follows:

$$WF = \sum_{i=1}^{T} CF_i \left(\frac{d_i}{D} \right)$$

where

CF_i = The ith addition or withdrawal
D = Total number of calendar days during the period
d_i = Number of days from the date of addition or withdrawal to the end of the period
T = Number of additions and withdrawals

For the previous example, the return is 13.56 percent. First, the weighted cash flow of –131.87 is calculated as follows:

$WF = -500\,(60/91) + 1{,}200\,(15/91) = -131.87$

It is assumed that the withdrawal of $500 was made at the end of the day on May 1, 1995. Similarly, the addition of $1,200 is assumed to be invested at the end of the day on June 15, 1995.

Second, given the weighted cash flow of –131.87, the portfolio return of 13.56 percent is calculated as follows:

$$r = \left[\frac{6{,}360 - 5{,}000 - 700 + 0}{5{,}000 - 131.87} \right] \times 100 = 0.1356 = 13.56\%$$

While the modified Dietz algorithm represents an improvement over the original Dietz algorithm, the return is affected by the timing of the cash flows and the sizes of the cash flows. The return is sensitive to factors outside the control of the money manager. In other words, the money manager has no control over when investors make additional investments or withdrawals or over the sizes of the additional investments or withdrawals. Therefore, the modified Dietz algorithm would not be as appropriate as the cumulative time-weighted return for evaluating the performance of the money manager.

Original Bank Administration Institute Method

Like the Dietz algorithm, this method assumes that net additions (additions minus withdrawals) occur at midpoint of the period. The rate of return is the value of r in the following equation that equates the compounded future values of the beginning value and the net addition to the ending value. The r in the equation is really the internal rate of return.

$$BV \times (1 + r) + NA \times (1 + r)^{1/2} = EV$$

where

BV = Beginning value
r = Internal rate of return
NA = Net additions = Additions – Withdrawals
EV = Ending value

For the example just given, the original BAI method yields a return of 12.36 percent. Given the net addition of $700 (1,200 – 500), the rate of return is calculated by trial and error. The value of 12.36 percent satisfies the following equation:

$$5,000 (1 + r) + 700 (1 + r)^{1/2} = 6,360$$

One drawback of this method is that it does not recognize the exact timing of cash flows. It assumes that the net addition occurs at the midpoint of the period.

Modified Bank Administration Institute Method

The modified BAI method recognizes the timing of cash flows explicitly and, therefore, represents an improvement over the original BAI formula. The rate of return is the value of r that satisfies the following equation:

$$BV\,(1+r) + \sum_{i=1}^{T} CF_i\,(1+r)^{(d_i/D)} \;=\; EV$$

where

BV = Beginning value

r = Internal rate of return

CF_i = Cash flows = Additions or withdrawals

d_i = Number of calendar days from the date of cash flow to the end of the period

D = Total number of calendar days in the period

EV = Ending value

For the previous example, the modified BAI method yields a return of 13.566 percent. Here again, this number is determined by trial and error and satisfies the following equation:

$$5{,}000(1 + r) - 500(1 + r)^{60/91} + 1{,}200(1 + r)^{15/91} = 6{,}360$$

Although this method addresses the timing of cash flows, the rate of return is affected by the sizes of cash flows and the timing of cash flows. For this reason, it is not as appropriate as the time-weighted return.

ANNUALIZING PORTFOLIO RETURNS

The methods just described can be used to calculate returns on a monthly, quarterly, or other period basis. If monthly or quarterly returns are available, the monthly or quarterly returns then can be annualized by adding one to each return, multiplying them together, and subtracting one.

Example.   Consider the following quarterly returns:

Quarter	1	2	3	4
Return (%)	12	−2	10	6

The annualized return (AR) is 27.98 percent:

$$AR = (1 + 0.12)(1 - 0.02)(1 + 0.1)(1 + 0.06) - 1 = 0.2798$$

RISK-ADJUSTED RETURNS

Often, high returns are associated with high levels of risk. For this reason, one should not judge a portfolio's performance by just looking at its return. It is also important to consider the risk level.

In this section, we look at three measures of return that adjust for risk. The risk-adjusted measures of returns are the reward-to-variability ratio, the reward-to-volatility ratio, and the Jensen measure.

The Reward-to-Variability Ratio

The reward-to-variability ratio also is called the *Sharpe ratio*. It is given by the following formula:

$$SR = (PR - RFR)/PSD$$

where

    SR = Sharpe ratio
    PR = Portfolio return
    RFR = Risk-free rate
    PSD = Portfolio standard deviation

This measure is appropriate if this portfolio represents the investor's only investment. In this situation, the standard deviation would be an appropriate measure of risk.

The higher the Sharpe ratio, the better. If this ratio for the portfolio is higher than the Sharpe ratio for the market, you could say the portfolio has outperformed the market.

    Example.   Consider the following data:

Average portfolio return	9%
Average Treasury bill rate	4%
Portfolio standard deviation	0.25

Sharpe ratio = (9% – 4%)/0.25 =   20%

The Reward-to-Volatility Ratio

The reward-to-volatility ratio also is called the *Treynor ratio*. It is calculated as follows:

$TR = (PR - RFR)/\text{beta}$

where

TR = Treynor ratio
PR = Portfolio return
RFR = Risk-free rate

As explained in Chapter 17, beta is a measure of the portfolio return's volatility relative to the market's return. It indicates the magnitude of a portfolio's systematic or market risk.

The higher the Treynor ratio, the better. If the portfolio's Treynor ratio is higher than the excess of the market return over the risk-free rate, you could say the portfolio has outperformed the market. The market's Treynor ratio is equal to the difference between the market return and the risk-free rate. This is because the market return's beta is equal to one.

The Treynor measure is appropriate if the investor has substantial other investments in addition to this portfolio. In such a situation, the use of beta as a measure of risk would be appropriate. Beta reflects the portfolio's systematic risk and not the total risk.

Example. Consider the following data:

Average portfolio return	9%
Average Treasury bill rate	4%
Portfolio beta	1.25

Treynor ratio = $(9\% - 4\%)/1.25$ = 4%

The Jensen Measure

The Security Market Line postulates that the expected return of a portfolio should be equal to

$EPR = RFR + \text{beta}\,(MR - RFR)$

where

EPR = Expected portfolio return
RFR = Risk-free rate
MR = Market return

The difference between the actual and the expected portfolio return is called *alpha*. If the actual portfolio return exceeds the expected portfolio return, alpha is positive and the portfolio has outperformed the market. If alpha is negative, the market has outperformed the portfolio.

SELECTED REFERENCES

Association for Investment Management and Research. *Report of the Performance Presentation Standards Implementation Committee.* December 1991.

Fabozzi, F. J. *Investment Management.* Englewood Cliffs; NJ: Prentice Hall, 1995.

Frailey, F. W. "How to Tell How You Are Doing." *Changing Times,* January 1988, pp. 37–42.

Kolb, R. W. *Investments.* Miami: Kolb Publishing Company, 1992.

Maginn, J. L., and D. L. Tuttle, eds. *Managing Investment Portfolios: A Dynamic Process.* Boston: Warren, Gorham & Lamont, 1990.

Sharpe, W. F., G. J. Alexander, and J. V. Bailey. *Investments.* Englewood Cliffs, NJ: Prentice Hall, 1995.

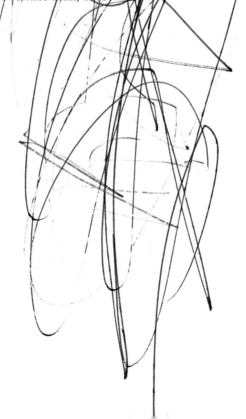

Chapter Nine

Real Estate Investment Returns

There are different types of real estate. They include residential properties, commercial properties, and industrial properties. The returns from investments in such properties consist of cash flows from operations and/or gains from the sales of the properties.

TYPES OF YIELDS

This chapter covers different measures of return on investments in income-producing real estate such as apartment buildings, office buildings, and shopping centers. The measures include the free and clear return, the equity dividend rate, the cash on cash return, the internal rate of return, the financial management rate of return, and the modified internal rate of return.

Free and Clear Return

The free and clear return is the amount of net operating income per dollar of total investment, assuming that the property is owned free and clear. Even if debt is used to acquire a real property, the free and clear return can be calculated by dividing the net operating income of the property by the sum of equity and debt.

Example. Consider the following data:

Potential gross income	$ 2,500,000.00
Vacancy costs	125,000.00
Operating expenses	1,000,000.00
Debt service	822,217.37
Property value	10,000,000.00
Debt	7,000,000.00
Equity	3,000,000.00

The free and clear return is 13.75 percent. It is calculated as follows:

Year	1
Potential gross income	$2,500,000.00
− Vacancy costs	−125,000.00
= Effective gross income	2,375,000.00
− Operating expenses	−1,000,000.00
= Net operating income	1,375,000.00
− Debt service	−822,217.37
= Before-tax cash flow	$ 552,782.63

$$\text{Free and Clear Return} = \text{NOI}/\text{Total Investment}$$
$$= 1,375,000/10,000,000$$
$$= 0.1375$$

The potential gross income is the product of the number of units in the building and the rent per unit. It measures the total rental income that the building can generate when all the units are leased. To the extent that some of the units are not leased, there are vacancy costs. There also may be collection costs. Both the vacancy and collection costs are subtracted from the potential gross income to get the effective gross income.

Operating expenses are subtracted from the effective gross income to get the net operating income. Operating expenses include management fees, repair and maintenance, telephone, advertising, transportation, property taxes, and insurance.

The free and clear return is easy to calculate. However, it does not take into account taxes, the time value of money, all cash flows from operations, and gains or losses from the sale of the real property. Furthermore, it does not measure return on equity. It reflects return on total investment, including debt.

Equity Dividend Rate

The equity dividend rate is a measure of the rate of return on equity. It is the ratio of before-tax cash flow in the first year to the investor's equity. For the example in the preceding section, the equity dividend rate is 18.43 percent. It is calculated as follows:

Potential gross income	$2,500,000.00
− Vacancy costs	−125,000.00
= Effective gross income	2,375,000.00
− Operating expenses	−1,000,000.00
= Net operating income (NOI)	1,375,000.00
− Debt service	−822,217.37
= Before-tax cash flow	552,782.63
÷ Equity	÷3,000,000.00
= Equity dividend rate	0.1843

If there is an outstanding loan, the debt service (i.e., principal and interest payment) should be subtracted from the net operating income to get the before-tax cash flow. When the before-tax cash flow is divided by the owner's equity investment, the result is the equity dividend rate.

The equity dividend rate also is easy to calculate but it is not a satisfactory measure of return. It does not take into account all the cash flows from operations and cash flows from the sale of the property. Nor does it take into account income taxes and the time value of money.

Cash on Cash Return

The cash on cash return does reflect income taxes. It is the ratio of after-tax cash flow in the first year to the investor's equity.

Example. Consider the following data:

Potential gross income	$ 2,500,000.00
Vacancy costs	125,000.00
Operating expenses	1,000,000.00
Debt service	822,217.37
Property value	10,000,000.00
Debt	7,000,000.00
Equity	3,000,000.00

Interest	$700,000.00
Depreciation	227,848.10
Marginal tax rate	0.31

For this example, the cash on cash return is 13.81 percent. It is calculated as

Potential gross income	$2,500,000.00
- Vacancy costs	-125,000.00
= Effective gross income	2,375,000.00
- Operating expenses	-1,000,000.00
= Net operating income (NOI)	1,375,000.00
- Interest	-700,000.00
- Depreciation	-227,848.10
= Taxable income	447,151.90
× Marginal tax rate	× 0.31
= Income tax	138,617.09
Net operating income	$1,375,000.00
- Debt service	-822,217.37
= Before-tax cash flow	552,782.63
- Income tax	-138,617.09
= After-tax cash flow	414,165.54
÷ Equity	÷3,000,000.00
= Cash on cash return	0.1381

While the cash on cash return takes into account income taxes, it does not reflect all cash flows from operations, cash flows from the sale of the real property, and the time value of money.

Internal Rate of Return

The internal rate of return (IRR) is one of the most widely used measures of return in the real estate field. It also is used in other investments such as stocks, bonds, and capital expenditures. The effective yield of a stock and the yield to maturity of a bond investment are, actually, internal rates of return.

The IRR is the rate of discount that equates the cost of an asset to the present value of the cash inflows generated by the asset. For example, if an asset is purchased for $1,000 today and then sold for $1,200 a year from now, the IRR would be 20 percent (1,200/1,000 − 1). However, the calculation of the IRR for a real estate investment is much more involved than this. Consider the following data:

Year	0	1	2
Before-tax cash flow	−3,000,000	552,782.63	4,139,639.11
− Taxes	−0	−138,617.09	−386,033.65
= After-tax cash flow	−3,000,000	414,165.54	3,753,605.46

Before-tax IRR = 27.04%
After-tax IRR = 19.76%

The IRR is calculated by trial and error. For example, the after-tax IRR is the value of y in the next equation, which equates the equity investment on the left side (cash flow in year 0) to the present value of the cash flows on the right side. The value of y that equates the two sides is 19.76 percent. This is the after-tax IRR. Similarly, the before-tax IRR is 27.04 percent. It is based on the before-tax cash flows.

$$3,000,000 = \frac{427,580.10}{(1+y)^1} + \frac{3,790,963.55}{(1+y)^2}$$

In this two-year example, the IRR also can be determined using the quadratic formula. For longer periods, however, the trial-and-error procedure or the Newton-Raphson procedure has to be used.

IRR: A case study.   A fairly detailed example demonstrates the computation of the IRR. Consider the following apartment building data:

Cost of building	=	$9,000,000
Land	=	1,000,000
Number of units	=	200
Annual rent per unit	=	12,500
Vacancy costs	=	5%
Operating expenses (percent of potential gross income)	=	40%
Straight-line depreciation rate	=	1/39.5
Equity investment	=	3,000,000
Loan amount	=	7,000,000
Loan term in years	=	20
Amortization	=	20
Annual interest rate of the loan	=	10%
Holding period in years	=	2
Estimated annual increase in property value	=	4%
Estimated annual increase in unit rent	=	4%
Investor's marginal tax rate	=	28%
Selling expenses as percent of selling price	=	5%

Before-tax cash flow from operations.

Year	1	2
Potential gross income	$2,500,000.00	$2,600,000.00
− Vacancy costs	−125,000.00	130,000.00
= Effective gross income	2,375,000.00	2,470,000.00
− Operating expenses	−1,000,000.00	−1,040,000.00
= Net operating income	1,375,000.00	1,430,000.00
− Debt service	−822,217.37	−822,217.37
= Before-tax cash flow	$ 552,782.63	$ 607,782.63

Taxes from operations.

Year	1	2
Net operating income	$1,375,000.00	$1,430,000.00
− Interest	−700,000.00	−687,778.26
− Depreciation	−227,848.10	−227,848.10
= Taxable income	447,151.90	514,373.64
× Marginal tax rate	×0.28	×0.28
= Income tax	$ 125,202.53	$ 144,024.62

Reversion: After-tax cash flow from sale.

Original cost of property	$10,000,000.00
− Accumulated depreciation	−455,696.20
+ Improvements	+0
= Adjusted basis of property	$ 9,544,304.80
Selling price	$10,816,000.00
− Selling expenses	−540,800.00
= Net selling price	10,275,200.00
− Adjusted basis	−9,544,303.80
= Capital gain	730,896.20
× Marginal tax rate	×0.28
= Tax on capital gain	$ 204,650.94
Net selling price	$10,275,200.00
− Loan balance	−6,743,343.52
= Before-tax cash flow	3,531,856.48
− Tax on capital gain	−204,650.94
= After-tax cash flow from sale	$ 3,327,205.54

Summary of after-tax cash flows.

Year	0	1	2
Before-tax cash flow	$–3,000,000	$552,782.63	$4,139,639.11
– Taxes	–0	–125,202.53	–348,675.56
= After-tax cash flow	$–3,000,000	$427,580.10	$3,790,963.55
Before-tax IRR = 27.04%			
After-tax IRR = 19.76%			

Weaknesses of the IRR.   The IRR is widely used in evaluating real estate and other investments. However, the IRR has some serious weaknesses. First, it assumes that cash flows are reinvested at the same rate as the IRR. The IRR is a measure of the rate of return of a particular project but it is not necessarily the rate of return that an investor would earn on reinvested cash flows. Some analysts believe that a different rate should be used for calculating earnings on reinvested cash flows before the IRR is calculated.

Second, the IRR may not exist. If it does not exist, it cannot be used. This problem may arise in a situation in which the initial cash flow is positive followed by a negative cash flow and then followed by a positive cash flow.

Third, there may be multiple IRRs. This situation arises when the annual cash flows switch from negative to positive and then to negative, and so on. According to Descarte's rule of signs, there could be as many IRRs as the number of sign changes in the cash flows. When the IRR is not unique, the IRR cannot be used.

Since the likelihood of alternating positive and negative cash flows is quite high in practice, the possible existence of multiple IRRs is a major problem. To overcome this problem, a number of alternative measures of return have been proposed. We consider the financial management rate of return (FMRR) and the modified internal rate of return (MIRR).

Financial Management Rate of Return

In the calculation of the IRR, cash flows from the project are assumed to be reinvested at the project's IRR. This assumption may not be realistic. So, two rates are used in the computation of the FMRR. The first rate, called the *safe rate* or the *conservative rate,* is used to compound positive cash flows forward to offset negative cash flows and to discount remaining negative cash flows back to the beginning of the project. It also is used to compound positive cash flows that are not needed to offset future negative cash flows forward until a predetermined amount is accumulated. Once the predetermined amount is accumulated, the positive cash flows are compounded forward to the end of the project's holding period at the second rate, called the *risk rate* or the *market rate.*

Once the negative cash flows that are not offset by positive cash flows in prior years are discounted back to the beginning of the project's holding period and positive cash flows that are not needed to offset future negative cash flows are compounded forward to the end of the holding period, the FMRR is calculated as the rate of return that equates the present value of the negative cash flows at the beginning of the holding period to the future value of the positive cash flows at the end of the holding period.

The formula for calculating the FMRR is

$$FMRR = \left[\frac{FV}{PV}\right]^{1/n} - 1$$

where

FV = Future values of the positive cash flows at the end of the project's term. These cash flows are not needed to offset negative cash flows during the term of the project.

PV = The inital cost plus the present values of all the negative cash flows that were not offset by prior positive cash flows

n = Investment horizon in years

Although the FMRR is calculated the way it is described in the preceding paragraphs, in our next example it will be modified slightly to simplify the calculation. Specifically, all positive cash flows that are not used to offset negative cash flows are compounded forward to the end of the project's term at the risk rate. The accumulation of a predetermined amount is ignored.

Example.   Consider the following cash flows:

Year	0	1	2	3	4
Cash flow	−2,000	1,500	−2,100	6,000	−1,050
Safe rate = 5%					
Risk rate = 10%					

First, the $1,500 positive cash flow in year 1 is invested at the safe rate of 5 percent to partially offset the negative cash flow of $2,100 in year 2. At 5 percent, the $1,500 grows to $1,575 by year 2. This amount is applied to the $–2,100 and the remaining cash flow is $–525. The present value of this amount at 5 percent is $–476.19. This amount is added to the initial cost of $2,000 so that the total cash flow in year 0 is $–2,476.19.

Second, a portion of the $6,000 cash flow in year 3 is used to pay for the $–1,050 cash flow in year 4. To determine the portion of the $6,000 needed to cover the $–1,050 cash flow, we divide −1,050 by 1 plus the safe rate of 5 percent and get $1,000. In other words, when $1,000 of the $6,000 in year 3 is invested at 5 percent, it grows to $1,050 by year 4 and that offsets the negative cash flow in year 4 fully.

Third, the $5,000 from year 3 that was not needed to cover the negative cash flow in year 4 is invested at the risk or market rate of 10 percent. At 10 percent, the $5,000 grows to $5,500 by year 4.

Finally, the FMRR is calculated as follows:

$$FMRR = \left[\frac{5,500}{2,476.19} \right]^{1/4} - 1 = 0.2208, \text{ or } 22.08\%$$

Weaknesses of the FMRR. The FMRR has a number of weaknesses. First, the required calculations are cumbersome although the use of computers eases the computational burden. Second, some people argue that the use of two rates, the safe rate and the risk rate, is not appropriate. They argue that only one rate that reflects the riskiness of the project's cash flows should be used. Furthermore, investing positive cash flows at a safe rate when there may be better investment opportunities does not seem appropriate. Third, depending on which positive cash flows prior to the negative cash flows are used to offset negative cash flows, there may be different FMRRs. This problem may not apply if only positive cash flows immediately preceding negative cash flows are used to offset negative cash flows. If the positive cash flows in the preceding year are not sufficient to cover the negative cash flow, then positive cash flows from the year prior to the preceding year would be used and so on.

Modified Internal Rate of Return

The modified internal rate of return (MIRR) also is used to overcome the possible nonuniqueness of the IRR. Like the FMRR, it uses two rates—the safe rate and the risk rate, but it is easier to calculate. The calculation of the MIRR requires the following steps:

Step 1. Discount the project's negative cash flows to the present using the safe rate.

Step 2. Compound the project's positive cash flows forward to the end of the project's holding period using the risk rate.

Step 3. Calculate the MIRR using the following formula:

$$MIRR = \left[\frac{FV}{PV}\right]^{1/n} - 1$$

where

FV = Future values of the positive cash flows at the end of the project's term

PV = The inital cost plus the present values of all the negative cash flows

n = Investment horizon in years

Example. Consider the example used in the previous section:

Year	0	1	2	3	4
Cash flow	–2,000	1,500	–2,100	6,000	–1,050

Safe rate = 5%
Risk rate = 10%

Step 1. Present values of negative cash flows at 5 percent.

$$-2,000 - \frac{2,100}{(1+0.05)^2} - \frac{1,050}{(1+0.05)^4} = -4,768.60$$

Step 2. Future values of positive cash flows at 10 percent.

1,500 $(1 + 0.10)^3$ + 6,000 $(1 + 0.10)$ = 8,596.50

Step 3. Calculate the MIRR.

$$MIRR = \left[\frac{8,596.50}{4,768.60} \right]^{1/4} - 1 = 0.1587, \text{ or } 15.87\%$$

Strengths and weaknesses of the MIRR. The calculation of the MIRR is easier than that of the FMRR and it eliminates the nonuniqueness problem of the IRR. However, the appropriateness of the use of two rates—the safe rate and the risk rate—is in question.

SUGGESTED READINGS

Alvin, A. *Real Estate Investor's Deskbook.* Boston: Warren, Gorham & Lamont, 1982.

Dilmore, G. *Quantitative Techniques in Real Estate Counseling.* Lexington; MA: Lexington Books, 1981.

Fisher, J. D., and R. S. Martin. *Income Property Valuation.* Chicago: Dearborn Financial Publishing, 1994.

Johnson, L. L., and J. A. Fellows. "Maximizing After-Tax Returns in the World of Passive Losses." *Real Estate Review,* Summer 1993, pp. 29–33.

Kerr, H. S. "A Final Word on FMRR." *The Appraisal Journal,* January 1980, pp. 95–103.

Little, J. F. "Is IRR Overrated?" *Real Estate Today,* June 1985, pp. 22–26.

Loesch, D. "Start with the Basics." *Real Estate Today,* January 1984, pp. 50–59.

Messner, S. D., and M. C. Findlay III. "Real Estate Investment Analysis: IRR versus FMRR." *The Real Estate Appraiser,* July/August 1975, pp. 5–20.

Tappan, Jr., W. T. *Handbook for the Financial Analysis of Real Estate Investments.* New York: McGraw-Hill, 1993.

Young, M. S. "FMRR: A Clever Hoax." *The Appraisal Journal,* July 1979) pp. 359–69.

Returns on Life Insurance

There are different types of insurance products. They include automobile insurance, homeowner's insurance, health insurance, disability insurance, and life insurance policies. This chapter covers returns on life insurance policies.

Life insurance is an important component of financial planning. It provides an immediate estate. For this reason, it is vital for people who have dependents but who haven't had a chance to accumulate wealth to purchase life insurance.

The basic types of life insurance policies are term insurance, whole life, universal, variable life, and universal variable life policies. With the exception of term policies, all the other products have some kind of a savings element.

A portion of the premium paid by the insured is used to cover mortality costs, and administrative and other expenses. The rest of the premium is invested. As a result, the policy accumulates a cash value that can be withdrawn, borrowed, or left to grow on a tax-deferred basis. If the insured dies, the beneficiary receives only the death benefit, not the cash value.

Term insurance is pure insurance. It provides protection only for the beneficiary when the insured dies.

TYPES OF RETURNS

Next we present four measures of return: the yearly rate of return, the rate of return on surrender, the rate of return on death, and the Linton yield.

Yearly Rate of Return

The yearly rate of return is calculated by comparing the costs and benefits of cash value life insurance. The cost of the insurance at the beginning of the period is the cash surrender value at the beginning of the year plus the premium for the policy. The benefit at the end of the year consists of the cash surrender value, any dividends received and the cost of protection against death. If there is an outstanding policy loan and the interest rate on the policy loan is smaller than the interest rate that can be earned on other investments, the difference between the interest earned on the investment and the interest cost of the loan would be part of the total benefit of the cash value insurance policy.

The yearly rate of return is useful for investors deciding whether to keep the cash value insurance policy in force or to terminate it. The yearly rate of return is calculated using the following formula:

$$r = \frac{CV_t + D_t + P_T (WF - CV_t)(0.001) + L(i_m - i_k)}{CV_{t-1} + P_W} - 1$$

where

r	=	Yearly rate of return
CV_t	=	Cash surrender value in year t
D_t	=	Dividends in year t
P_T	=	Term insurance premium rate
WF	=	Whole life insurance face amount
L	=	Outstanding policy loan
i_m	=	Market interest rate
i_k	=	Interest rate on policy loan
CV_{t-1}	=	Cash surrender value in year $t-1$
P_W	=	Whole life insurance annual premium

Example. Consider the following whole life insurance data:

Face amount	=	$100,000
Annual premium	=	1,200
Policy loan amount	=	1,000
Policy loan rate	=	5%
Return on invested policy loan	=	8%

Year	Cash Surrender Value	Dividends	Cost of Term per $1,000
1996	6,600	100	3.10
1997	8,100	105	3.25

The yearly rate of return is 9.41 percent. It is calculated as

$$r = \frac{8,100 + 105 + 3.25(100,000 - 8,100)(0.001) + 1,000(0.08 - 0.05)}{6,600 + 1,200} - 1$$

Rate of Return on Surrender

A policyowner can surrender the policy for the cash value in the policy by surrendering the policy. The rate of return on the surrender of the policy is the rate of return that equates the future value of the annual premiums to the cash surrender value at a specified time in the future. The rate of return on surrender is calculated by trial and error using the following equation:

$$CSV_N = P_W \times \left[\frac{(1+r)^N - 1}{1 - (1+r)^{-1}}\right]$$

where

CSV_N = Cash surrender value in year N
N = Number of years to the date of surrender
P_W = Annual whole life premium
r = Rate of return on surrender

Example. Consider the following whole life insurance policy data:

Face amount	$50,000.00
Annual premium	1,000.00
Year of surrender	10
Cash surrender value	$12,486.35

Dividends are used to purchase additional life insurance. The rate of return on surrender is 4 percent. This rate satisfies the following equation:

$$12{,}486.35 = 1{,}000 \times \left[\frac{(1+r)^{10} - 1}{1 - (1+r)^{-1}} \right]$$

The problem with this measure of return is that it is based on illustrations supplied by the insurer. Often times, the illustrations or projections are not accurate. They may be based on falling expenses and mortality costs, rising interest rates, and policy terminations. These assumptions produce attractive illustrations but they may not hold, much to the disappointment of the policyholders.

Rate of Return on Death

The main reason for buying life insurance is to provide death benefits to beneficiaries on the death of the insured. The rate of return on death or the rate of return to the beneficiary is calculated using the same procedure as that used in the calculation of the rate of return on surrender. It is the rate of return that equates the future value of the annual premiums to the death benefit. The rate is calculated by trial and error using the following equation:

$$DB_N = P_W \times \left[\frac{(1+r)^N - 1}{1 - (1+r)^{-1}} \right]$$

where

DB_N = Death benefit in year N
N = Number of years to the date of death
P_W = Annual whole life premium
r = Rate of return on death

Example. Consider the following life insurance policy data:

Death benefit	$50,000
Annual premium	900
Year of death	1

Dividends are used to purchase additional life insurance. In this case, the rate of return can be easily calculated:

$$r = [(50{,}000/900) - 1] \times 100 = 5{,}455.56\%$$

The rate of return is high because the beneficiary collected $50,000 after only one premium payment of $900. As the time to death gets longer, the rate of return falls because the amount of premiums paid gets larger and the present value of the death benefit declines with time.

      Example.   Consider the following whole life insurance policy data:

Death benefit	$50,600
Annual premium	900
Year of death	5

Dividends are used to purchase additional life insurance. The rate of return is 95.34 percent. This rate satisfies the following equation:

$$50,600 = 900 \times \left[\frac{(1+r)^5 - 1}{1 - (1+r)^{-1}} \right]$$

Linton Yield

The Linton yield is the measure of return used in the context of "buy term and invest the difference." Since the premium of a whole life policy is initially higher than the premium of a term policy with the same face amount, some people argue that instead of buying whole life, an individual can buy term insurance and invest the difference between the whole life premium and the term premium to build a separate fund.

The sum of the fund and the face value of the term insurance are supposed to be equal to the face value of the whole life. For this reason, as the investment fund grows, the face amount of the term insurance is reduced.

The Linton yield is the rate of return on the invested premiums that produces a fund equal to the whole life cash value by the end of a designated time.

Before the Linton yield can be determined, the following calculations have to be performed:

1. Determine the face amount of the term insurance policy.

$$TFA_t = (WFA - WP + D_t - F_{t-1}) / [1 - (TR_t \times 0.001)]$$

where

TFA_t = Term face amount in policy year t
WFA = Whole life face amount
WP = Whole life annual premium
D_t = Whole life dividend in year t
F_{t-1} = Investment fund in year $t-1$
TR_t = Term rate per \$1,000 of face amount in year t

2. Determine the term insurance premium (TP_t).

$$TP_t = TR_t \times 0.001 \times TFA_t$$

3. Determine the premium invested (PI_t).

$$PI_t = WP - D_t - TP_t$$

4. Determine the investment fund (IF_t) using a trial rate.

$$IF_t = (IF_{t-1} + PI_t) \times (1 + r)$$

where

r = Trial interest rate

The Linton yield is determined then by trial and error.

Example. Consider the following data:

Whole life face amount   \$250,000
Cash value in year 5   12,877
Whole life annual premium   3,010

Policy year	1	2	3	4	5
Term rate/1000	2.27	2.38	2.55	2.71	2.92

The Linton yield is 2.5 percent. This is the rate that produces an investment fund equal to the cash value of the whole life insurance by the end of year 5. In year 5, both are equal to \$12,877. See Table 10–1.

Once the Linton yield is determined, it can be compared with rates on alternative investments. If those rates are higher than the Linton yield, buying term and investing the difference may be better than whole life.

TABLE 10–1
Calculation of the Linton Yield

	Whole Life Face Amount			$250,000		
	Cash Value in Year 5			12,877		
	Whole Life Annual Premium			3,010		

Policy Year	Term Rate	Term Amount	Term Premium	Premium Invested	Fund BOY	Fund EOY
0						0
1	2.27	247,552	562	2,448	2,448	2,509
2	2.38	245,064	583	2,427	4,936	5,059
3	2.55	242,549	619	2,391	7,450	7,637
4	2.71	240,003	650	2,360	9,997	10,247
5	2.92	237,437	693	2,317	12,564	12,877

The problem with the Linton yield is that it is based on illustrations or projections made by the insurer; these projections on the ledger statements may lack accuracy.

SELECTED REFERENCES

Baldwin, B. G., and W. G. Droms. *The Life Insurance Investment Advisor.* Chicago: Probus Publishing, 1988.

Belth, J. M. "The Rate of Return on the Savings Element in Cash-Value Life Insurance." *The Journal of Risk and Insurance*, December 1968, pp. 569–81.

Black, K., Jr., and H. Skipper, Jr. *Life Insurance.* Englewood Cliffs, NJ: Prentice Hall, 1987.

Brownlie, W. D, and J. L. Seglin. *The Life Insurance Buyer's Guide.* New York: McGraw-Hill, 1989.

Daily, G. "Whole Life Policies: How to Evaluate One You Own." *AAII Journal*, May 1987, pp. 25–28.

Davis, K. "Buying Life Insurance: What the Numbers Don't Show." *Kiplinger's Personal Finance Magazine*, June 1994, pp. 49–52.

Dorfman, M. S., and S. W. Adelman. *The Dow Jones-Irwin Guide to Life Insurance.* Burr Ridge, IL: Dow Jones-Irwin, 1988.

_____. *Life Insurance: A Financial Planning Approach.* Chicago: Dearborn Financial Publishing, 1992.

Chapter Eleven

Yields of Mortgage-Backed Securities

Mortgage loans are originated by lenders such as savings and loan associations, commercial banks, and mortgage banks. Lenders originating loans for their own portfolios are called *portfolio lenders* and those that originate loans but do not plan to keep the loans in their portfolios are called *secondary lenders*. The secondary lenders may sell the loans to secondary market agencies—the Federal National Mortgage Association (Fannie Mae) and the Federal Home Loan Mortgage Corporation (Freddie Mac)—or they may form pools of mortgages and issue securities backed by the mortgage pools. They also may swap their mortgages with Fannie Mae mortgage-backed securities or Freddie Mac mortgage participation certificates. The Fannie Mae mortgage-backed securities and the Freddie Mac mortgage participation certificates are securities backed by mortgages and their cash flows are guaranteed by Fannie Mae and Freddie Mac respectively.

TYPES OF MORTGAGE-BACKED SECURITIES

There are two major types of mortgage-backed securities. They are mortgage pass-through securities and mortgage-backed derivative securities. In the first case, securities backed by a pool of mortgages are issued and sold to investors. The payments (cash flows) to the investors may be guaranteed by the Government National Mortgage

Association (Ginnie Mae), Fannie Mae, Freddie Mac, or a private entity.

The mortgage servicers collect the monthly mortgage payments from the home owners, deduct servicing and guarantee fees, and forward the rest of the payments to the investors. The investors are paid on a pro rata basis.

In the second case, two or more classes of securities backed by pools of mortgages or mortgage pass-throughs are created and principal and/or interest payments are allocated to different classes of securities. Within the derivatives category, there are Collateralized Mortgage Obligations (CMOs) or Real Estate Mortgage Investment Conduits (REMICs) and Stripped Mortgage-Backed Securities (SMBSs).

CMOs are multiclass derivatives. The classes have different stated maturities. For example, if a CMO has four classes of securities (A, B, C, and Z), owners of securities A, B, and C would receive interest on the payment dates but the interest on the class Z security would not be paid to the investors. Instead, the interest would simply accrue and be added to the face amount. In addition, owners of class A security would receive all the scheduled principal payment and any principal prepayments until they are completely paid off. After the class A securities are retired, all principal payments go to the owners of class B securities until class B securities are retired, and so on. This way, the prepayment risks are reduced for owners of class B, C, and Z securities.

The second kind of mortgage-backed derivative is the stripped MBS. The stripped MBS may be a Principal Only (PO) strip or an Interest Only (IO) strip. All the principal payments from the underlying security are allocated to the PO and all the interest payments are allocated to the IO.

This chapter presents measures of yields on mortgage pass-throughs.

TYPES OF MBS YIELDS

Only two measures of yield are introduced here. The first measure is the cash flow yield and the second one is the bond-equivalent yield. The latter is based on the former.

Cash Flow Yield

The cash flow yield is the discount rate that equates the present value of the monthly cash flows from the mortgage pass-through security to the price paid for the security. The monthly cash flows consist of interest, scheduled principal payments, and any prepayments allocated to the mortgage pass-through security unit. The face amount of a unit is normally $25,000 but the price of the unit depends on market conditions.

Example. Suppose the price of a unit pass-through is $24,500. The remaining cash flows are as follows:

Year	Cash Flow ($)	Year	Cash Flow ($)
1	$2,192.28	7	2,198.63
2	2,196.62	8	2,194.99
3	2,199.67	9	2,189.99
4	2,201.41	10	2,183.61
5	2,201.82	11	2,175.85
6	2,200.90	12	2,166.70

Monthly cash flow yield	=	1.11%
Annualized cash flow yield	=	13.32%
Compounded annual cash flow yield	=	14.16%

The annualized cash flow yield is the monthly yield times 12 and the compounded annual cash flow yield is calculated by adding 1 to the monthly yield, raising the sum to the power of 12, and subtracting 1 from the result.

Bond-Equivalent Yield

The cash flows from a mortgage pass-through are received monthly whereas the coupon payments of a bond typically are received semiannually. The bond-equivalent yield of the mortgage pass-through is comparable or equivalent to the yield of a bond. It is calculated as

$$BEY = 2 \times [(1 + MCFY)^6 - 1]$$

where

BEY = Bond-equivalent yield
$MCFY$ = Monthly cash flow yield

For the example in the previous section, the bond-equivalent yield is 13.7 percent, calculated as follows:

$$BEY = 2 \times [(1 + 0.0111)^6 - 1] = 0.137, \text{ or } 13.7\%$$

The Wall Street Journal reports cash flow yields of mortgage-backed securities in section 3. The cash flow yields are based on Salomon Brothers' prepayment model.

SUGGESTED READINGS

Carron, A. "Understanding CMOs, REMICs, and Other Mortgage Derivatives." *Journal of Fixed Income*, June 1992, pp. 25–43.

Fabozzi, F. J. *Investment Management*. Englewood Cliffs, NJ: Prentice Hall, 1995.

Fabozzi, F. J., and F. Modigliani. *Mortgage & Mortgage-Backed Securities Markets*. Boston: Harvard Business School Press, 1992.

Haydre, L. S., and C. Mohebbi. "Mortgage Pass-Through Securities." In *Bond & Mortgage Markets*, ed. F. J. Fabozzi. Chicago: Probus Publishing, 1989.

Chapter Twelve

Bank Loans

The funds (deposits) that banks receive from their patrons are used primarily to finance consumer loans, business loans, and real estate loans. This chapter shows the calculations of the yields on these types of bank loans.

CONSUMER LOANS

Banks make credit card loans, loans that are paid back at the end of the loan term in one lump-sum, and installment loans. In installment loans, the bank makes a lump-sum payment to the borrower at the time of origination and the borrower repays the loan in equal installments over a specified time. This section presents a formula for approximating the annual percentage rate (APR) of an installment loan.

Annual Percentage Rate (APR)

The APR is the true cost of credit. This is the rate that the lender has to disclose to the borrower. The calculation of the APR requires a trial-and-error procedure. However, a simplified formula can be used to approximate it. The approximate formula for calculating the APR is

$$APR = \frac{2 \times m \times F}{L(n+1)}$$

where

APR = Approximate annual percentage rate
m = Number of periods in a year

L = Loan amount
n = Total number of scheduled payments
F = Finance or interest charges

Example.   Helen borrows $10,000 to buy a car. She plans to repay the loan in 48 equal monthly installments of $253.63. The total interest cost of the loan is $2,174.24. The approximate APR for this loan is

$$APR = \frac{2 \times 12 \times 2{,}174.24}{10{,}000(48 + 1)} = 0.1065, \text{ or } 10.65\%$$

Add-on Rate

The add-on rate is a simple interest rate used to calculate the total interest cost of the loan. However, if the monthly loan payment, the number of payments, and the loan amount are known, the total interest cost of the loan can be determined as follows:

$$F = M \times n - L$$

where

F = Total interest cost
M = Monthly payment
n = Total number of payments
L = Loan amount

Given the total interest cost and the term of the loan in years, the add-on rate can then be calculated using the following formula:

$$i = \frac{F}{L \times t}$$

where

i = Add-on rate per year
t = Term of the loan in years

For the preceding example, the total interest cost is

$$F = 253.63 \times 48 - 10{,}000 = 2{,}174.24$$

The corresponding add-on rate is

$$i = \frac{2{,}174.24}{10{,}000 \times 4} = 0.054356$$

The true APR is the rate of discount that equates the present value of the monthly payments to the loan amount. For the prior example, the APR is 10 percent.

BUSINESS LOANS

Banks offer a variety of loans to businesses. They offer short-term and long-term loans, as well as secured and unsecured loans. Examples of secured loans are accounts receivable loans and inventory loans; examples of unsecured loans are lines of credit and revolving credits. In both lines of credit and revolving credits, the bank approves specific credit limits for the borrower. However, the bank makes a legal commitment to allow the borrower to use funds up to the credit limit only if it is a revolving credit. For this commitment, it charges a commitment fee. In lines of credit, the bank does not have the legal commitment to make funds available up to the credit limit.

The yields on business loans depend on whether interest is computed on a simple interest basis or discount basis and on whether the bank requires compensating balances or not. If interest is calculated on a simple interest basis and there is no compensating balance requirement, the effective yield is the same as the simple interest rate. The effective yield exceeds the simple interest rate if there is discount interest, a compensating balance requirement, or both. In any case, the effective yield is the ratio of the dollar amount of the interest cost to the net borrowed funds.

Discount loan. In a discount loan, the bank collects the interest in advance and the net borrowed funds equal the loan amount less the discount interest. The effective yield of the discount loan is equal to

$$EY = I/NBF = i/(1-i)$$

where

EY = Effective yield
I = Interest
NBF = Net borrowed funds
i = Simple interest rate

Example.   Suppose a company needs to borrow $200,000 for a year. The bank charges 10 percent in advance. How much should it borrow and what is the effective yield?

The amount of the loan should be

$L = $ Amount needed$/(1 - i) = 200,000/(1 - .10) = 222,222.22$

The interest amount is

$I = L \times i = 222,222.22 \times 0.10 = 22,222.22$

The effective yield on the loan is

$EY = I/NBF = 22,222.22/200,000 = 0.1111$

or

$EY = i/(1 - i) = 0.10/(1 - 0.10) = 0.1111$

Simple Interest Loan with Compensating Balance

In addition to collecting interest at the end of the year, the bank may require the borrower to open a noninterest-bearing checking account and keep a specified percentage of the loan amount in the account while the loan is outstanding. The interest is calculated on the entire loan amount but the amount available to the borrower is the face amount of the loan less the compensating balance required. The compensating balance requirement increases the effective yield of the loan. The effective yield of this type of loan is equal to

$EY = I/NBF = i/(1 - cb)$

where

EY = Effective yield
I = Interest
NBF = Net borrowed funds
i = Simple interest rate
cb = Compensating balance requirement

Example.   Suppose a company needs to borrow $200,000 for a year. The bank charges 10 percent and requires a 20 percent compensating balance. How much should it borrow and what is the effective yield?

The amount of the loan should be:

$L = \text{Amount needed}/(1 - cb)$

$= 200,000/(1 - 0.20) = 250,000.00$

The interest amount is

$I = L \times i$

$= 250,000.00 \times 0.10 = 25,000.00$

The effective yield on the loan is

$EY = I/NBF$

$= 25,000/200,000 = 0.125$

or

$EY = i/(1 - cb)$

$= 0.10/(1 - 0.20) = 0.125$

Discount Interest Loan with Compensating Balance

For a discount interest loan with compensating balance, the lender collects interest in advance. In addition, the bank requires a compensating balance. Here also, the interest is calculated on the entire loan amount but the amount available to the borrower is the face amount of the loan less the sum of the discount interest and the compensating balance required.

The effective yield of this type of loan is equal to

$$EY = I/NBF = i/(1 - cb - i)$$

where

EY = Effective yield
I = Interest
NBF = Net borrowed funds
i = Simple interest rate
cb = Compensating balance requirement

Example.   Suppose a company needs to borrow $200,000 for a year. The bank charges 10 percent in advance and requires a 20 percent compensating balance. How much should it borrow and what is the effective yield?

The amount of the loan should be

$$L = \text{Amount needed}/(1 - cb - i)$$

$$= 200,000/(1 - 0.20 - 0.10) = 285,714.29$$

The interest amount is

$$I = L \times i$$

$$= 285,714.29 \times 0.10 = 28,571.43$$

The effective yield on the loan is

$$EY = I/NBF$$

$$= 28,571.43/200,000 = 0.1429$$

or

$$EY = i/(1 - cb - i)$$

$$= 0.10/(1 - 0.20 - 0.10) = 0.1429$$

REAL ESTATE LOANS

Banks make residential as well as commercial real estate loans. The commercial real estate loans include land development and construction loans. However, this section deals only with the calculation of the effective yield or annual percentage rate (APR) on a residential real estate loan.

Before explaining the calculation of the effective yield, we must remind you that a point is 1 percent of the loan amount. For example, if the loan amount is $100,000, a point would be 1 percent of $100,000, or $1,000. This amount ($1,000) is paid by the borrower at closing. If the borrower does not cover the point by paying cash at closing, the lender would deduct $1,000 from the loan amount of $100,000 and disburse only $99,000. The point represents interest paid in advance (i.e., discount interest). This discount interest is in addition to the interest paid monthly by the borrower. Thus, the effective yield on the loan is higher than the interest rate on the mortgage loan. The greater the number of points, the bigger the difference between the interest rate on the mortgage loan and the effective yield on the loan.

Example. Consider the following data:

Loan amount	$100,000
Annual interest rate	8.25%
Term (years)	30
Monthly mortgage payment	$751.27
Discount points	2.3

Since the number of discount points is 2.3, the amount of the discount interest is $2,300 and the proceeds of the loan, $97,700 (100,000 – 2,300).

The effective yield on the loan is the rate of discount that equates the present value of the 360 monthly payments of $751.27 to the loan proceeds of $97,700 at closing. The effective yield is 8.5 percent.

If the lender expects the borrower to pay off the loan in five years, the lender can earn the same effective yield of 8.5 percent by charging only one point ($1,000) at closing.

Annual Percentage Rate

The annual percentage rate (APR) is the rate that lenders have to disclose when making mortgage loans. It is the effective yield on a mortgage loan. In addition to discount points and the monthly interest that the borrower has to pay during the term of the loan, it reflects other items such as loan origination fees, prepaid interest (also called *interest adjustment*), and private mortgage insurance (PMI).

The calculation of the APR is similar to the calculation described in the previous section. All the finance charges paid at closing, not just the discount points, have to be subtracted from the loan amount to get the net loan amount at closing. To the extent that private mortgage insurance premiums are spread over the term of the loan, the premiums have to be added to the monthly mortgage payments.

The APR is the rate of discount that equates the present value of the monthly payments (including the PMI premiums) to the difference between the loan amount and the finance charges (i.e., to the net loan amount) at closing.

SUGGESTED READINGS

Brigham, E. F. *Fundamentals of Financial Management*. Ft. Worth, TX: Dryden Press, 1992.

Brueggeman, W. B., and J. D. Fisher. *Real Estate Finance & Investments*. Burr Ridge, IL: Richard D. Irwin, 1993.

Camsey, B. J., and E. F. Brigham. *Introduction to Financial Management*. Ft. Worth, TX: Dryden Press, 1991.

Piches, G. E. *Essentials of Financial Management*. New York: Harper-Collins, 1992.

Yohannes, A. G. *Real Estate Finance*. Columbus, OH: Greyden Press, 1994.

Chapter Thirteen

Returns on Capital Expenditures

Capital expenditures are expenditures on the tangible long-term assets of a business entity. They may be expenditures on land, buildings, or machinery and equipment.

There are five criteria for evaluating proposed capital expenditures. They are the payback method, the average rate of return method, the net present value method, the internal rate of return method, and the profitability index. These criteria reflect the returns from the proposed capital expenditures.

PAYBACK METHOD

The payback is the number of years it takes a project to recover the original investment in the project. The shorter the payback the better. When using the payback, the company may specify a maximum payback and accept proposed projects only if their paybacks are shorter than the specified payback.

Example. Consider the following cash flow data for two proposed projects, A and B:

Year	0	1	2	3
Cash flow of A	−1,000	250	600	1,500
Cash flow of B	−1,200	900	700	200

The company's maximum payback requirement is two years.

The payback of project A is 2.1 years. The project recovers $850 in the first two years. Since the project generates $1,500 in the third year, the remaining $150 of the original investment is recovered in one-tenth of the third year. Thus, it takes project A 2.1 years to recover the original investment of $1,000. Since the maximum payback for the company is two years, the project is rejected. However, the payback of Project B is 1.43 years. It is accepted.

The payback method is easy to use but it suffers from two major weaknesses. First, it ignores the time value of money. It assumes that a dollar today has the same value as a dollar in the future, when in fact its value declines with time. Second, it favors projects with quick returns. It ignores cash flows beyond the company's maximum payback. This means it could reject projects that in the long run would have been more profitable than the projects that it accepts. In the previous example, Project A is more profitable than Project B over the three-year period, but the payback method selected Project B. However, note that the longer the time into the future, the less reliable the forecasts tend to be. That is why the focus is on quick returns.

AVERAGE ACCOUNTING RATE OF RETURN METHOD

There are different versions of the average accounting rate of return (AARR) method. The version used here is the ratio of the average net income (profit after taxes) to the initial investment. The higher the ratio, the better the project. The company may also specify a critical rate for accepting or rejecting a proposed project. If the project's AARR is higher than the specified rate, it is accepted; otherwise, it is rejected.

Example. Consider the following data:

Year	0	1	2	3
Investment	1,500	—	—	—
Net income		600	650	700

$$AARR = \frac{\dfrac{(600 + 650 + 700)}{3}}{1,500} = 0.867, \text{ or } 86.7\%$$

The AARR method is easy to use. It also uses the net incomes for the entire period of the project. However, it ignores the time value of money and the timing of net incomes. Furthermore, it uses net incomes and not cash flows.

NET PRESENT VALUE METHOD

The net present value (NPV) of a project is the difference between the present values of the cash inflows and the present values of the cash outflows. A proposed project is accepted if its NPV is positive; it is rejected if its NPV is negative. The higher the NPV, the more acceptable the proposed project will be.

Example. Consider the following data for a proposed project:

Year	0	1	2	3
Cash flows	−1,000	250	600	1,400

Required rate of return = 15%

The NPV of this project is $657.35. Since this amount is positive, the project is accepted.

The NPV method takes into account the time value of money. It also uses all the projected cash flows of the proposed project. However, it requires the specification of the required rate of return (cost of capital) in advance. Nonetheless, it is believed to be the most appropriate method for evaluating capital expenditures.

INTERNAL RATE OF RETURN METHOD

The internal rate of return (IRR) is the rate of discount that equates the present values of the future cash flows to the initial cost of the project. It is also the rate of discount that makes the net present value equal to zero.

A proposed project is accepted if the IRR of the project exceeds the required rate of return. The higher the IRR, the better. A proposed project is rejected if the IRR is smaller than the required rate of return.

Example.   Consider the following data for a proposed project:

Year	0	1	2	3
Cash flows	−1,000	250	600	1,400

This project's IRR is 41.85 percent. It is the rate of discount that equates the present values of the cash flows in years 1, 2, and 3 to the initial investment (cash outflow) of $1,000. It is calculated using a trial-and-error procedure.

The IRR is a widely used criterion for selecting investment projects for the following reasons:

• It takes into account the time value of money.
• It takes into account all the cash flows of the proposed project.

However, it has some serious weaknesses also. The weaknesses are

• It assumes a reinvestment rate that is equal to the IRR. Cash flows are assumed to be reinvested at a rate equal to the IRR. This may not be the case in practice.

• The IRR may not be unique. In other words, there may be multiple IRRs if there are multiple changes in the signs of the cash flows. According to Descartes's rule of signs, the number of IRRs can be as many as the number of sign changes. When this happens, the IRR criterion cannot be used.

• The IRR may not exist. It may not be possible to find a rate of discount that makes the NPV equal to zero. In this case, the IRR criterion breaks down completely.

• When the sizes of two alternative projects under consideration are different, the choice of the IRR method may conflict with that of the NPV criterion. In this case and in all other cases where there is a conflict between the IRR method and the NPV method, the NPV method should be used.

PROFITABILITY INDEX

The profitability index (PI) is the ratio of the present values of the positive cash flows to the present values of the negative cash flows. A project is accepted if the PI is greater than one and it is rejected if the PI is less than one. The higher the PI, the better.

Example. Consider the following data for a proposed project:

Year	0	1	2	3
Cash flows	−1,000	250	600	1,400

Since the present value of the positive cash flows is $1,657.35, the PI for this proposed project is 1.657 (=1,657.35/1,000). This project is acceptable, because the PI is greater than one.

Like the NPV and the IRR criteria, the PI method also takes into account the time value of money and uses all the cash flows of the proposed project.

However, when two or more projects with different sizes are under consideration, the PI method may select projects that are different from the projects selected by the NPV method. In this case, the NPV method should be used.

SUGGESTED READINGS

Block, S. B., and G. A. Hirt. *Foundations of Financial Management*. Burr Ridge, IL: Richard D. Irwin, 1994.

Kaen, F. *Corporate Finance*. Cambridge, MA: Blackwell Publishers, 1995.

Ross, S. A.; R. W. Westerfield; and J. F. Jaffe. *Corporate Finance*. Burr Ridge, IL: Richard D. Irwin, 1993.

Shetty, A. G.; F. J. McGrath; and I. M. Hammerbacher. *Finance: An Integrated Global Approach*. Burr Ridge, IL: Richard D. Irwin, 1995.

Van Horne, J. C. *Financial Management & Policy* Englewood Cliffs, NJ: Prentice Hall, 1995.

Chapter Fourteen

Measures of Business Profitability

Financial ratios are used to evaluate the profitability, liquidity, asset utilization, and debt position of a business entity. This chapter reviews the measures of business profitability. Because the financial ratios are constructed using items from the balance sheet and the income statement, we begin by briefly discussing these two statements.

FINANCIAL STATEMENTS

Of the three major types of business financial statements—the income statement, the balance sheet, and the statement of cash flows—only the first two are reviewed here.

Balance Sheet

The balance sheet shows the assets, liabilities, and net worth of a business as of a specific point in time, such as December 31, 1995. The assets consist of current assets and long-term assets. The current assets are expected to be converted into cash within a year or within the operating cycle of the business. Examples are cash and equivalents, accounts receivable, marketable securities, and inventory.

The long-term assets include land, buildings, and machinery and equipment. They may be grouped under property, plant, and equipment. Other long-term assets include intangible assets such as patents and copyrights.

TABLE 14–1
Balance Sheet of Alpha, Inc. ($ in millions)

	December 31	
	1996	*1995*
Assets		
Cash and equivalents	$ 20	$ 20
Accounts receivable	150	145
Inventory	100	90
Other current assets	5	5
Total current assets	275	260
Property, plant, and equipment (net)	470	460
Total assets	$745	$720
Liabilities		
Accounts payable	$100	$ 90
Wages payable	22	23
Taxes payable	23	20
Other current liabilities	5	2
Total current liabilities	150	135
Long-term liabilities	250	250
Total Liabilities	$400	$385
Stockholders' Equity		
Par value of common stock	$ 50	$ 50
Surplus	85	85
Retained earnings	210	200
Total stockholders' equity	345	335
Total liabilities and equity	$745	$720

The liabilities also are broken down into current liabilities, such as accounts payable, wages payable, and taxes payable, and long-term liabilities, such as bonds payable and mortgages payable.

The net worth is the difference between total assets and total liabilities. For business corporations, it includes the par value of common stocks, surplus, and retained earnings. It may also include preferred stocks. For corporations, net worth is called stockholders' equity. Table 14–1 shows a balance sheet for a hypothetical company called Alpha, Inc.

TABLE 14–2
Income Statement of Alpha, Inc.

		December 31	
For the year ended:		1996	1995
	Gross sales	$1,000	$800
−	Returns and discounts	5	4
=	Net sales	995	796
−	Cost of goods sold	500	396
=	Gross profit or margin	495	400
−	Operating expenses	295	210
=	Operating income or profit	200	190
−	Interest	10	10
=	Earnings before taxes	190	180
−	Income taxes	40	37
=	Net income	150	143

Income Statement

The income statement shows the revenues, expenses, and net income of a business entity over a defined period. The income statement can be prepared for a month, a quarter, a year, and so forth. Table 14–2 shows an income statement for a hypothetical company called Alpha, Inc.

MEASURES OF PROFITABILITY

The profitability of a company is of interest to the owners of the company as well as to the creditors of the company. To show the profitability of the business, analysts use several measures. Here, we present and discuss four measures: the rate of return on net sales, also called the *after-tax profit margin;* the rate of return on assets; the rate of return on equity; and earnings per share.

Rate of Return on Sales

The rate of return on sales (ROS) measures the after-tax profit per dollar of net sales. It is calculated by dividing net income for the year by net sales for the same year. The higher the rate of return on sales, the better.

For Alpha, Inc., the rate of return on sales for 1996 is

ROS = Net income/Net sales = 150/995 = 0.1508, or 15.08%

By rewriting the ROS formula, it is possible to identify the factors that affect the rate of return on sales. The ROS formula can be rewritten as

$$ROS = \frac{NI}{EBT} \times \frac{EBT}{OI} \times \frac{OI}{NS}$$

where

NI = Net income
EBT = Earnings before taxes
OI = Operating income
NS = Net sales

The first ratio (NI/EBT) shows the tax effect or the burden of the tax, the second ratio (EBT/OI) shows the effect of interest or the interest burden, and the third ratio (OI/NS) shows operating efficiency and the extent to which the company is able or not able to command premium prices for its products. The operating efficiency indicates how well costs are controlled by the company.

Rate of Return on Assets

The assets of the business are financed by equity and debt. The rate of return on assets (ROA) measures the return to the suppliers of equity and debt. The rate of return on assets also measures the productivity of the assets of the business. It is calculated by dividing the sum of net income and interest expense by average total assets, where the average total assets is the sum of the total assets of the company at the beginning of the year and the total assets at the end of the year divided by two. The higher the rate, the better. The ROA for Alpha, Inc., is

$$ROA = \frac{\text{Net income} + \text{Interest}}{\text{Average total assets}} = \frac{150 + 10}{732.50} = 0.2184, \text{or } 21.84\%$$

Rate of Return on Equity

The rate of return on equity (ROE) is the after-tax profit per dollar of common equity. It is the ratio of net income to the average of common equity at the beginning of the year and common equity at the end of the year. If the company has preferred stocks outstanding, preferred dividends are subtracted from net income before it is divided by common equity. Obviously, the higher the ROE, the better. For Alpha, Inc., the ROE is

$$ROE = \text{Net income} / \text{Average common equity} = 150/340 = 0.4412$$

Here again, the determinants of the ROE can be identified by rewriting the ROE formula as follows:

$$ROE = \frac{NI}{EBT} \times \frac{EBT}{OI} \times \frac{OI}{NS} \times \frac{NS}{TA} \times \frac{TA}{E}$$

where

TA = Total assets
E = Equity

The ratio of total assets to equity (TA/E) shows financial leverage, the extent to which total assets are financed by equity and debt. The next ratio, the ratio of net sales to total assets (BS/TA), is the total assets turnover and it shows the productivity of total assets in terms of generating sales. The other ratios were explained earlier. They show the productivity of sales in generating profits after accounting for taxes and the interest burden.

Earnings per Share

Earnings per share (EPS) is a widely used ratio. Generally accepted accounting principles (GAAP) require that EPS be disclosed on the income statement. The earnings per share is the amount of after-tax profits per share. It is calculated by dividing net income less pre-ferred dividends by the number of common shares outstanding. This type of EPS is called the undiluted EPS. If the corporation has warrants and convertible bonds or convertible preferred stocks, two other types of EPS are calculated. They are the primary EPS and the fully diluted EPS. The primary EPS takes into account common stock equivalents and the fully diluted EPS reflects common stock equivalents as well as other convertible securities.

For Alpha, Inc., the average number of shares for the year is 100 and the undiluted EPS is

EPS = Net income/Average number of shares outstanding

= 150/100 = 1.50

USING RATIOS

The ratios by themselves may not be meaningful. To make them meaningful, the user has to compare them with historical values of the ratios for the same company or with industry norms. For example, a rate of return on equity of 15 percent may appear impressive. However, if all the other companies in the industry have ROEs of more than 20 percent, 15 percent would not be as impressive.

Industry norms can be obtained from Robert Morris Associates, *Annual Statement Studies*, and Dun & Bradstreet Credit Services, *Industry Norms and Key Business Ratios*, among other sources.

SUGGESTED READINGS

Bodie, Z.; A. Kane; and A. J. Marcus. *Essentials of Investments*. Burr Ridge, IL: Richard D. Irwin, 1995.

Fabozzi, F. J. *Investment Management*. Englewood Cliffs, NJ: Prentice Hall, 1995.

Fraser, L. M. *Understanding Financial Statements*. Englewood Cliffs, NJ: Prentice Hall, 1995.

Fridson, M. S. *Financial Statement Analysis*. New York: John Wiley & Sons, 1995.

Gibson, C. H. *Financial Statement Analysis*. Boston: PWS-Kent Publishing, 1989.

Gordon, G. *Understanding Financial Statements*. Cincinnati, OH: South-Western Publishing, 1992.

Hirt, G. A, and S. B. Block. *Fundamentals of Investment Management*. Burr Ridge, IL: Richard D. Irwin, 1993.

Maness, T. S., and J. W. Henderson. *Financial Analysis & Forecasting*. Englewood Cliffs, NJ: Prentice Hall, 1991.

Weston, J. F., and T. E. Copeland. *Managerial Finance*. Ft. Worth, TX: Dryden Press, 1992.

Chapter Fifteen

Types of Risk

Practically, there are no investments without risk. Even the investments that appear to be completely risk-free are exposed to some kind of risk. For example, Treasury securities are considered to be the safest investments. They are free of default risk but they are not free of interest rate risk or inflation risk.

To understand risk, the investor has to understand the different types of risk. They include default risk, interest rate risk, market risk, inflation risk, financial risk, business risk, illiquidity risk, and foreign exchange rate risk.

DEFAULT RISK

Default risk is the risk that the issuer of a debt instrument, such as a bond, will not pay the semiannual interest payments or the face value at maturity. With United States government securities, the risk of default is practically nonexistent. With debt instruments issued by businesses and state and local governments, however, there is always some risk. The level of risk varies from issuer to issuer.

Since it is difficult for investors to evaluate the risk associated with a particular corporate or municipal bond, investors rely on the ratings assigned to bonds by commercial rating services such as Standard & Poor's and Moody's Investor Services. There are several grades or levels of ratings. For example, Standard & Poor's assigns AAA to the bond with the highest rating, AA to the next highest rating, A for the third highest, and BBB for the fourth highest rating, and so on. Bonds rated BBB or higher are called *investment grade bonds*, and bonds rated BB or lower are called *junk bonds*.

In general, bonds with high ratings have lower yields than bonds with low ratings. In states that have no income taxes, the difference between the yield on a Treasury bond and the yield on a corporate bond with the same maturity would be an estimate of the size of the default risk associated with that particular bond. For example, if the yield on a 30-year Treasury bond is 8 percent and the yield on a 30-year, BBB-rated corporate bond is 12 percent, the implied default risk of the corporate bond would be roughly 4 percent.

INTEREST RATE RISK

Interest rate changes affect the value of financial assets such as bonds. When interest rates go up, bond values go down; when interest rates go down, bond values go up. In other words, interest rates and bond values are inversely related. The risk of loss resulting from interest rate fluctuations is called *interest rate risk*.

Although values of all bonds go down when interest rates go up, values of bonds with longer terms and lower coupon or interest payments go down more than the values of shorter-term, higher-coupon bonds. In other words, the interest rate risk of a long-term, low-coupon bond is higher than the interest rate risk of a short-term, high-coupon bond. If interest rates are expected to go up, the appropriate investment strategy would be to switch from long-term, low-coupon bonds to short-term, high-coupon bonds to minimize losses. The opposite strategy would be appropriate if interest rates are expected to go down. The latter strategy would maximize gains.

Even Treasury bonds are affected by swings in interest rates. The Treasury cannot guarantee that losses from interest rate increases will not occur if you sell before maturity.

MARKET RISK

Returns on individual stocks may be affected by movements in the stock market in general. Market risk refers to the volatility of stock returns resulting from the volatility of the market. This type of risk is not unique to a specific stock. It affects stocks in general and it cannot be diversified away by increasing the number of stocks in a portfolio. That is why it also is called *nondiversifiable risk*. The portion of total risk that can be diversified away is called *nonmarket risk* or *diversifiable risk*. It is unique or specific to a particular stock.

INFLATION RISK

Inflation reduces the purchasing power of money. As a result, it affects fixed-income securities adversely. Even Treasury securities that are free from default risk are not free of inflation risk. In times of inflation, both the interest payments and the face values decline in purchasing value.

This example shows the potentially devastating effect of inflation: If the annual inflation rate is 10 percent, an investor with $10,000 today would need $16,105.10 five years from now to buy the equivalent of $10,000 of goods today. The equivalent amount 10 years from now would be $25,937.42. Obviously, the equivalent amounts would be smaller if inflation is lower.

Annual inflation rate	=	10%
Current amount	=	$10,000
Equivalent amount five years from now	=	$16,105.10
Equivalent amount 10 years from now	=	$25,937.42

FINANCIAL RISK

Financial risk is the type of risk associated with the use of debt. Businesses can finance more assets by supplementing their equities with debt. The debt gives them more leverage. The debt also generates tax benefits. The interest on the debt is tax-deductible.

However, the use of excessive debt could also increase the risk of default. The business may not be able to honor its debt payments.

BUSINESS RISK

Business risk refers to the variability of operating income or operating profit of a business entity. The greater the variability of the income stream, the greater the level of business risk. Business risk affects the interest to bondholders and the dividends to the stockholders.

The level of business risk depends on the variability of sales and the existence of fixed costs of production. The greater the volatility of sales and the greater the amount of fixed costs relative to variable costs, the higher the level of business risk tends to be.

OTHER TYPES OF RISK

Other types of risk include illiquidity risk, callability risk, and foreign exchange risk. Some assets may be difficult to sell quickly. There also may be the risk of considerable losses from the sale of those assets. In other words, they may have substantial illiquidity risks. The illiquidity risks are generally due to limited markets. Examples would be interests in limited partnerships and shares of some closely held corporations.

Callability risk applies to callable securities such as callable preferred stocks and callable bonds. A corporation that issued a 20-year, callable bond may, for example, reserve the right to call back its bond anytime after a call protection period of, say, 5 years. That means investors who hold the bond after five years will be exposed to the risk of call. The issuer may call back the bond to lower interest costs or to retire some of its debts. If the issuer calls back the bonds when interest rates fall, investors would have to reinvest their funds at lower interest rates.

Investors who invest overseas face foreign exchange risks. Their investments may generate impressive returns. However, if exchange rates move against them, gains from their investments may be wiped out or reduced substantially.

SUGGESTED READINGS

Francis, J. C. *Management of Investments*. New York: McGraw-Hill, 1993.

Jones, C. P. *Investments*. New York: John Wiley & Sons, 1993.

Maginn, J. L., and D. C. Tuttle. *Managing Investment Portfolios*. Boston: Warren, Gorham & Lamont, 1990.

Mayo, H. B. *Investments*. Ft. Worth, TX: Dryden Press, 1994.

Reilly, F. K., and E. A. Norton. *Investments*. Ft. Worth, TX: Dryden Press, 1995.

Standard Deviation, Coefficient of Variation, and Semivariance

Over time, returns on investments fluctuate. As a result, investors are not able to tell in advance how much they will earn on their investments. The returns could be high or low; they could be positive or negative. The greater the variability, the greater the risk associated with the investment.

Statistical measures of variation are used to quantify risk. There are several statistical measures of variation. They include the range, the interquartile range, the mean deviation, the standard deviation, the coefficient of variation, and the semivariance. This chapter covers only the last three measures.

THE STANDARD DEVIATION

The standard deviation is probably the most widely used quantitative measure of risk. It measures the average degree of variability of individual returns around the expected or mean return.

Interpretation

If all the possible returns are equal to the mean return, the standard deviation is zero. That means the mean return is truly representative of all the possible returns. It is, in fact, equal to each one of them. The investor's return is equal to the mean.

However, if the possible returns vary considerably from the expected return, the standard deviation is high. The expected or mean return no longer is representative of the possible returns and the investor cannot expect to receive a return equal to the mean return. However, given the mean return and the standard deviation of the returns and assuming a normal distribution of returns, the investor can determine the range of the expected return with a specified probability. Specifically, the following probability statements would apply:

- The probability that the return would be greater than the mean minus one standard deviation but less than the mean plus one standard deviation would be 68.3 percent. For example, if the mean return is 10 percent and the standard deviation of the returns is 2 percent, the investor can expect a return between 8 and 12 percent with a 68.3 percent probability.

- The probability that the return would be greater than the mean minus two standard deviations but less than the mean plus two standard deviations would be 95.4 percent. For example, if the mean return is 10 percent and the standard deviation of the returns is 2 percent, the investor can expect a return between 6 and 14 percent with a 95.4 percent probability.

- The probability that the return would be greater than the mean minus three standard deviations but less than the mean plus three standard deviations would be 99.7 percent. For example, if the mean return is 10 percent and the standard deviation of the returns is 2 percent, the investor can expect a return between 4 and 16 percent with a 99.7 percent probability.

Measurement

To estimate the standard deviation of possible returns, the probability distribution of future returns has to be known; that is, the possible returns and their associated probabilities. The probability distribution is difficult to determine. So, assuming that the actual observed or past returns represent the possible returns, historical data are used to show the calculation of the standard deviation and the other measures of risk.

Since the standard deviation is calculated using a sample, the sample standard deviation (SD) is calculated using the following formula:

$$SD = \left[\frac{(R_i - \mu)^2}{n-1} \right]^{1/2}$$

where

R_i = The ith return

μ = Mean return

n = Number of returns

The sample SD differs from the population in that the denominator of the sample SD is $n - 1$ while for the population SD, the denominator is simply n. In both cases, the standard deviation is the square root of the variance.

Example. Consider the following hypothetical data:

Year	1991	1992	1993	1994	1995
Return (5)	10	8	15	–2	25

The variance is 0.0097 (=0.0389/(5–1)) and the standard deviation is 9.86% (square root of 0.0097). It is calculated as follows:

Year	Return(R_i)	$R_i - \mu$	$(R_i - \mu)^2$
1991	0.10	–0.0120	0.0001
1992	0.08	–0.0320	0.0010
1993	0.15	0.0380	0.0014
1994	–0.02	–0.1320	0.0174
1995	0.25	0.1380	0.0190
Total	0.56		0.0389

$$\text{Mean return} = \mu = \frac{\sum R_i}{n} = \frac{0.56}{5} = 0.112, \text{ or } 11.2\%$$

$$SD = \left[\frac{0.0389}{5-1} \right]^{\frac{1}{2}} = 0.0986, \text{ or } 9.86\%$$

The standard deviation is widely used and it has nice statistical properties. However, it has some weaknesses also. First, it is based on the units of the original observation. It measures absolute variation. For this reason, it may not be appropriate to compare the variability of the returns of one stock with the variability of the returns of another stock. For example, if the standard deviation of the returns of ABC stock is 2 percent and that of XYZ stock is 4 percent, one cannot say that the XYZ stock is two times riskier than the ABC stock.

Second, the standard deviation is calculated using returns greater than the expected return as well as returns less than the expected return. Investors are not concerned about returns that are greater than the expected return. In fact, they like those returns. They are more concerned about returns less than the expected return or returns less than some target return. They would definitely be concerned about negative returns. In a situation like this, the standard deviation would not be appropriate.

THE COEFFICIENT OF VARIATION

The previous section pointed out that it is not appropriate to compare standard deviations of the returns of different stocks because the standard deviation is a measure of absolute deviation. To compare variabilities of the returns of two different stocks, you have to use a measure of relative dispersion. The coefficient of variation is such a measure.

The coefficient of variation is simply the ratio of the standard deviation of the return to the mean return. For the example in the previous section, the coefficient of variation is 0.88. It is calculated as follows:

$$CV = SD/\mu = 0.986/0.112 = 0.88$$

where

CV = Coefficient of variation
SD = Standard deviation
μ = Mean return

The coefficient of variation is easy to calculate. However, since it is based on the standard deviation, it shares one of the weaknesses of the standard deviation. It is based on returns greater than the mean return as well as returns less than the mean return, although investors are concerned only about the returns less than the mean return.

SEMIVARIANCE

The semivariance is also a measure of variation but it uses only returns less than the mean return or some other target return like zero percent. It focuses only on returns that fall below expectations. Thus positive deviations from the mean are ignored. Only negative deviations are used. Otherwise, the computational procedure is the same as that of the variance.

For the previous example, the semivariance is 0.0046, or 0.46 percent, calculated as follows:

Year	Return (R_i)	$R_i - \mu$	$(R_i - \mu)^2$
1991	0.10	−0.0120	0.0001
1992	0.08	−0.0320	0.0010
1993	0.15	0.0000	0.0000
1994	−0.02	−0.1320	0.0174
1995	0.25	0.0000	0.0000
Total	0.56		0.0185

$$\text{Mean return} = \mu = \frac{\sum R_i}{n} = \frac{0.56}{5} = 0.112, \text{ or } 11.2\%$$

Semivariance = $0.0185 / (5 - 1) = 0.0046$

Although the semivariance focuses on returns that fall below the expected return, it lacks the desirable properties that the standard deviation possesses. For example, the mean and the standard deviation describe the normal distribution and, as you saw, probability statements can be made about the possible returns of an investment. The same cannot be said of the semivariance.

PORTFOLIO RISK

The risk of a portfolio of securities is measured by the standard deviation of the portfolio. It depends on the proportions of funds invested in the individual securities that make up the portfolio, the standard deviation of each security, and the correlations between the returns of the securities. For a portfolio consisting of just two securities, the standard deviation of a portfolio is given by the following formula:

$$SD_P = \sqrt{X_A^2 \times SD_A^2 + X_B^2 \times SD_B^2 + 2X_AX_B \, R_{AB}SD_A SD_B}$$

where

SD_P = Standard deviation of the portfolio
X_A = Proportion of money invested in security A
X_B = Proportion of money invested in security B
SD_A = Standard deviation of security A
SD_B = Standard deviation of security B
SD_A^2 = Variance of security A
SD_B^2 = Variance of security B
R_{AB} = Correlation coefficient between security A and security B

Example. Consider the following data:

Proportion of money invested in security A	= 0.5
Proportion of money invested in security B	= 0.5
Standard deviation of security A	= 0.6
Standard deviation of security B	= 0.5
Variance of security A	$= 0.6^2 =$ 0.36
Variance of security B	$= 0.5^2 =$ 0.25
Correlation between security A and security B	= +1

The variance of the portfolio is 0.3025 and its square root, the standard deviation, is 0.55, calculated as

$$SD_P = \sqrt{(0.5^2 \times 0.6^2) + (0.5^2 \times 0.5^2) + (2 \times 0.5 \times 0.5 \times 1 \times 0.6 \times 0.5)} = 0.55$$

Since the correlation coefficient is +1, the returns of securities A and B are perfectly and positively correlated. The returns of the two securities move up or down at the same time. They behave the same way. Given this perfect positive correlation, investing in both security A and B is equivalent to investing in just A or B. When the correlation coefficient is one, there is no risk reduction or diversification.

However, if the correlation coefficient is smaller than one, it is possible to reduce the portfolio risk to a level lower than the risk level associated with each of the securities in the portfolio without lowering the expected return. The smaller the correlation coefficient value, the smaller the risk of the portfolio tends to be. In fact, when the securities in the portfolio are perfectly negatively correlated—that is, when the correlation coefficient is minus one—it is possible to reduce portfolio risk to zero. The loss from one security would be fully offset by a gain from another security in the portfolio.

For the prior example, the portfolio standard deviations corresponding to different values of the correlation coefficient are

Correlation coefficient	1	0	−1
Portfolio standard deviation	0.55	0.39	0.05

For a portfolio consisting of just two securities, the portfolio standard deviation is zero if the proportion of the investment budget that is invested in security A is equal to the ratio of the standard deviation of security B to the sum of the standard deviations of A and B. For the preceding example, the portfolio risk is zero if the proportion of money invested in security A is

$$X_A = \frac{SD_B}{SD_A + SD_B} = \frac{0.5}{0.6 + 0.5} = 0.4545$$

The proportion of money that has to be invested in B would be $1 - 0.4545$ or 0.5455.

SUGGESTED READINGS

Fischer, D. D., and R. J. Jordon. *Security Analysis & Portfolio Management.* Englewood Cliffs, NJ: Prentice Hall, 1995.

Francis, J. C. *Investments.* New York: McGraw-Hill, 1991.

Fuller, R. J., and J. L. Farrell, Jr. *Modern Investments & Security Analysis.* New York: McGraw-Hill, 1987.

Markowitz, H. M. *Portfolio Selection.* Cambridge, MA: Blackwell Publishers, 1991.

Reilly, F. F. *Investment Analysis & Portfolio Management.* Ft. Worth, TX: Dryden Press, 1994.

Sanders, D. H.; A. F. Murph; and R. J. Eng. *Statistics.* New York: McGraw-Hill, 1976.

Sharpe, W. F.; G. J. Alexander; and J. V. Bailey. *Investments.* Englewood Cliffs, NJ: Prentice Hall, 1995.

Chapter Seventeen

Beta

There are probably many factors that explain changes in security returns. One factor that is believed to affect the changes in security returns is the return on a broad market index. Beta measures the sensitivity of changes in the return of a security to changes in the market return. It is a measure of the volatility of the return of a security relative to that of the market.

If the return of a security is as volatile as the market return, its beta is one; it is equal to that of the market. If the market return increases by 10 percent, the return on the security also increases by 10 percent.

If the security's return is more volatile than that of the market return, the security's beta will be greater than one. For example, if the security's beta is 1.2, the security's return is 20 percent more volatile than the market return. That means when the market return increases by 10 percent, the security's return will increase by 12 percent. Securities with betas greater than one are riskier than the market and they are called *aggressive securities*.

On the other hand, if the security's return is less volatile than that of the market return, the security's beta is smaller than one. For example, if the security's beta is 0.9, the security's return is 10 percent less volatile than the market return. That means when the market return increases by 10 percent, the security's return increases by only 9 percent. Securities with betas smaller than one are less risky than the market and they are called *defensive securities*.

MEASUREMENT OF BETA

Beta is estimated using a statistical technique called *regression* and a simple linear model representing what is called a *characteristic line*. The model is

$$R_i = a + b(MR_i) + e_t$$

where

R_i = Return of a particular security in period i

MR_i = Return on a market index, usually the Standard & Poor's 500 Stock Index

a = Constant term

b = Beta

e_i = Error term

The constant term (a) is calculated using the following formula:

$$a = \frac{\Sigma R}{n} - b \frac{\Sigma MR}{n}$$

Beta is calculated using the following formula:

$$b = \frac{n\Sigma(MR)(R) - \Sigma MR \, \Sigma R}{n\Sigma MR^2 - n\,(\Sigma MR)^2}$$

where

n = Number of observations

Some practical problems have to be dealt with when estimating data. First, should an analyst use historical data to estimate beta? Assuming that the historical relationship between the security's return and the market return holds in the future, historical return data may be used to estimate beta. However, beta does not seem to remain stable over time due to estimation errors and due to changes in factors that are not explicitly included in the estimation equation.

Second, what is the appropriate period for computing returns? In other words, should the analyst use weekly returns, monthly returns, or quarterly returns? Any of these periods may be used. Some firms use weekly returns; others use monthly returns.

Third, how long should the period for estimation be? Should it be two years, three years, four years, or five years? Any one of these periods may used.

Fourth, what is the appropriate market index? Is it the Dow-Jones Industrial Average, the Standard & Poor's 500 Stock Average, the

New York Stock Exchange composite index, or some other index? The appropriate market index is an index that includes all assets. However, since such an index does not exist, broad indexes such as the Standard & Poor's index are used.

Thus, the beta value for a security could vary depending on the type of data used, the estimation period, and the market index used. Nonetheless, it is still useful because it indicates the degree of relative risk or volatility of the security's return.

Example. Consider the following hypothetical data:

Year	Return of Stock A (%)	Market Return (%)
1992	10%	8%
1993	8	10
1994	15	14
1995	-2	-5
1996	25	26

To calculate beta and the constant term (a), the table can be expanded as follows:

Year	R_i	MR_i	R_iMR_i	MR^2
1992	10	8	80	64
1993	8	10	80	100
1994	15	14	210	196
1995	-2	-5	10	25
1996	25	26	650	676
	56	53	1,030	1,061

Mean value of $R = 56/5 = 11.2\%$

Mean value of $MR = 53/5 = 10.6\%$

Beta is 0.874, calculated as follows:

$$b = \frac{(5)(1,030) - (53)(56)}{(5)(1,061) - 53^2} = 0.874$$

The constant term (a) is 1.933, calculated as follows:

$$a = \frac{56}{5} - 0.874 \left(\frac{53}{5}\right) = 1.933$$

PORTFOLIO BETA

Once the betas of individual securities are calculated, portfolio beta can be determined using the security betas. Specifically, the beta of a portfolio is the weighted average of the betas of the individual securities that make up the portfolio, where the weights are proportions of funds invested in the securities.

Example. Consider the following data:

Value of portfolio	=	$50,000
Amount invested in security A	=	20,000
Amount invested in security B	=	30,000
Beta of security A	=	1.2
Beta of security B	=	0.9

Portfolio beta = $(0.4)(1.2) + (0.6)(0.9)$ =   1.02

BETA AND TOTAL RISK

The variance or its square root, the standard deviation, measures the total risk of a stock investment. The total risk consists of systematic risk and nonsystematic risk. Systematic risk, also called *market risk* or *nondiversifiable risk*, depends on economywide factors such as inflation and taxes that tend to affect all stocks. For this reason, diversification does not reduce this type of risk.

Nonsystematic risk, also called *nonmarket risk, company-specific risk,* or *diversifiable risk,* depends on factors that apply to a particular firm and it can be diversified away or reduced by diversifying a portfolio. For example, suppose a portfolio includes stocks of two companies, A and B. If company A loses a major contract, its earnings may go down. However, if the contract is awarded to company B, the award may increase the earnings of company B, thereby offsetting the decline in the earnings of company A. In a portfolio containing stocks of company A and company B, diversification would reduce the nonsystematic risk and the total risk.

In general, the size of the nonsystematic risk and the size of the total risk fall as the number of securities in a portfolio increases. The decline in nonsystematic risk and total risk depends on the correlation among the returns of the securities in the portfolio.

The correlation coefficient shows the degree of association among the returns. Its value ranges from a low of negative one (called perfect negative correlation) to a high of plus one (called perfect positive correlation). Diversification reduces risk as long as the correlation coefficient is less than plus one. However, the smaller the correlation coefficient, the greater the risk reduction tends to be. If two security returns are highly negatively correlated, a fall in one return may be offset by the increase in the other return.

Systematic risk (SR) is measured using one of these formulas:

$$SR = R^2 \times (SD_A^2)$$

or

$$SR = \text{Beta}^2 \times (SD_M^2)$$

where

R^2	=	Coefficient of determination
SD_A^2	=	Variance of the return on security A
SD_M^2	=	Variance of the market return

The nonsystematic risk is the complement of systematic risk. It is one minus the systematic risk. Alternatively, it is one minus the coefficient of determination times the variance of the return of the stock.

The coefficient of determination is a measure of the goodness of fit of a regression model to a set of data. It shows the proportion of the total variation in the dependent variable that is explained by the independent variable. Its maximum value is one, or 100 percent, and its minimum value is zero. For example, if the computed R square (R^2) is 0.92, it means 92 percent of the variance of the dependent variable is explained by changes in the independent variable. The 8 percent is explained by other factors.

Example.   The following data are calculated from the return data for stock A and the market given earlier.

Population variance of the return of stock A $= SD_A^2 = 8.8408^2$ $=$ 78.16

Population variance of the market return $= SD_M^2 = 9.992^2$ $=$ 99.84

$R^2 =$ Coefficient of determination $=$ 0.9762

Beta $=$ 0.7642

Systematic risk	$= 0.9762 \times 78.16$	$=$ 76.30
or		
Systematic risk	$= 0.7642^2 \times 99.84$	$=$ 76.30
Nonsystematic risk	$= 78.16 - 76.30$	$=$ 1.86
or		
Nonsystematic risk	$= (1 - 0.9762) \times 78.16$	$=$ 1.86

BETA AND EXPECTED RETURN

The previous section pointed out that beta is a measure of systematic risk and that systematic risk cannot be reduced by diversifying a portfolio. Investors require compensation for the systematic risk that they have to bear but not for the diversifiable risk they can eliminate through efficient diversification.

Thus, beta could be used to determine the rate of return that investors expect on an investment. Specifically, the capital asset pricing model (CAPM) or the securities market line (SML) is used to determine the expected return on an investment. The formula for the SML is

$R_i = RFR + b(MR - RFR)$

where

R_i	$=$ Expected return on security i
RFR	$=$ Risk-free rate $=$ Rate on a Treasury bill
MR	$=$ Return on a market index
b	$=$ Beta $=$ Quantity of risk
$MR - RFR$	$=$ Price of risk

In the absence of risk, the investor's expected return is the risk-free rate. On a risky investment, however, the expected return would include a risk premium. The risk premium is the quantity of risk measured by beta times the price of risk (difference between the market return and the risk-free rate).

Example.   Consider the following data:

Risk-free rate   =   6%
Beta   =   1.2
Market return   =   8%

The investor's expected return would be 8.4 percent, calculated as follows:

$$R_i = 6\% + 1.2(8\% - 6\%) = 8.4\%$$

ADJUSTMENTS TO BETA

Over a period of years, the computed value of beta tends to move toward one. Values greater than one get smaller as they move toward one and values smaller than one get larger as they move toward one. Firms that calculate betas for different companies adjust betas to correct for this tendency.

CRITICISMS OF BETA

Some people argue that beta should be estimated using a market index that includes all assets, not just stocks. Since such an index does not exist, it is difficult to get an accurate value of beta. Furthermore, depending on the type of return data used, the estimation period chosen, and the market index selected, different people can get different beta values for the same company.

The correlation between beta and expected return is also in question. Some evidence suggests that a higher value of beta does not necessarily mean a higher expected return.

SUGGESTED READINGS

Blume, M. "Betas and Their Regression Tendencies." *Journal of Finance*, June 1975, pp. 785–95.

Fabozzi, F. J. *Investment Management*. Englewood Cliffs, NJ: Prentice Hall, 1995.

Fama, E. F., and K. R. French. "The Cross-Section of Expected Stock Returns." *Journal of Finance*, June 1992, pp. 427–65.

Fuller, R. J., and J. L. Farrell, Jr. *Modern Investments & Security Analysis*. New York: McGraw-Hill, 1987.

Hirt, G. A., and S. B. Block. *Fundamentals of Investment Management*. Burr Ridge, IL: Richard D. Irwin, 1993.

Newbold, G. D., and P. S. Poon. "The Minimum Number of Stocks Needed for Diversification." *Financial Practice & Education*," Fall 1993, pp. 85–87.

Reilly, F. K. *Investment Analysis & Portfolio Management*. Ft. Worth, TX: Dryden Press, 1994.

Sharpe, W. F.; G. J. Alexander; and J. V. Bailey. *Investments*. Englewood Cliffs, NJ: Prentice Hall, 1995.

Wagner, W. H., and S. C. Lau. "The Effect of Diversification on Risk." *Financial Analysts Journal*, November/December 1971, pp. 48–53.

Chapter Eighteen

Duration and Convexity

There is an inverse relationship between interest rates and security prices. If interest rates or yields go up, security prices go down, causing losses to investors; if interest rates go down, security prices go up, yielding gains to the owners of those securities. However, the responses of security prices to changes in interest rates are not the same for all securities. For example, prices of long-term bonds respond more to changes in interest rates than prices of short-term bonds. Also prices of low-coupon bonds are more sensitive to interest rate changes than prices of high-coupon bonds.

The investment implications for investors are the following:

- If interest rates are expected to go up, investors should switch from long-term, low-coupon bonds to short-term, high-coupon bonds to minimize losses.
- If interest rates are expected to go down, investors should switch from short-term, high-coupon bonds to long-term, low-coupon bonds to maximize gains.

DURATION

Duration is a measure of the sensitivity of the price of the bond to changes in yields or interest rates. It takes into account the three major factors that affect the relationship between the yields and fixed-income security prices. The three factors are the term to maturity of the security, the size of the coupon payment, and the level of yields or interest rates.

Duration is not the same as the term to maturity of a bond, although for zero-coupon bonds, the duration of the bond is equal

TABLE 18–1
Calculation of Macaulay's Duration

(1) Year	(2) Cash Flow	(3) DF @ 9%	(4)=(2)×(3) PV(CF)	(5)=(4)/P PV/Price	(6)=(5) × (1) Weighted Ratio
1	90	0.9174	82.57	0.08257	0.08257
2	90	0.8417	75.75	0.07575	0.15150
3	1,090	0.7722	841.68	0.84168	2.52504
			Price = 1,000.00		Duration = 2.75911

DF = Discount factor
PV(CF) = Present values of cash flows

to the term of the bond. For coupon bonds, however, duration is shorter than the term of the bond, simply because the investor does not have to wait until the end of the term of the bond to receive a dollar of cash flow.

Macaulay's Duration

The calculation of duration for a bond with a long term can be really cumbersome unless a spreadsheet program is used. To use a spreadsheet program, however, the user has to know the procedure for computing duration.

A short-term bond will be used to demonstrate the calculation of duration. See Table 18–1.

Example.   Consider the following bond data:

Face amount	=	$1,000
Annual coupon rate	=	9%
Term in years	=	3
Yield to maturity	=	9%

Since the coupon rate is 9 percent, the investor can expect to receive $90 each year. In addition, the investor will receive the face value of $1,000 at maturity. The investor's expected cash flows are shown in column (2) of Table 18–1.

Column (3) shows discount factors at the bond's yield to maturity. The discount factors are calculated as follows:

$$DF_t = \left(\frac{1}{1+i}\right)^t$$

where

DF_t = Discount factor in year t
i = Yield to maturity
t = Year

For example, for year 1, the discount factor is

$$DF_1 = 1/(1+0.09)^1 = 0.9174$$

Column (4) shows the present values of the cash flows. The present values are the products of the cash flows in column (2) and the discount factors in column (3). The sum of the annual cash flows yields the price of the bond.

Column (5) is generated by dividing the annual present values of the cash flows by the price of the bond.

Column (6) is the product of the years in column (1) and the ratios in column (5). The sum of the weighted ratios in column (6) is duration. This type of duration is called *Macaulay's duration.*

Modified Duration

Modified duration is based on Macaulay's duration. Macaulay's duration can be converted to modified duration as follows:

$$D_m = \text{Macaulay's duration}/(1+i)$$

where

D_m = Modified duration
i = Original yield to maturity

For the previous example, the modified duration is

$$D_m = 2.76/(1+0.09) = 2.53$$

Effective Duration

In the example both Macaulay's duration and modified duration were calculated with the assumption that the bond would be held until maturity. However, if a bond is callable, the bond may be called back prior to maturity. A shorter term such as the number of years to the first call date may be more appropriate than the number of years to maturity.

In the case of mortgage-backed securities, there is the risk of prepayments due to falling mortgage rates, job transfers, or unemployment. Thus, prepayments should be taken into account.

Effective duration takes into account both the callability risks of bonds and the prepayment risks of mortgage-backed securities. For this reason, effective duration would be a better indicator of risk than modified duration that would tend to overstate the risks associated with bonds and mortgage-backed securities.

Uses of Duration

Duration is useful for predicting changes in the prices of bonds and mortgage-backed securities. It is also useful in immunizing bond portfolios.

Predicting changes in bond prices. A popular rule of thumb is that the percentage change in the price of the bond is equal to the modified duration of the bond. For example, if the duration of the bond is five years, a 1 percent increase in interest rates would result in a 5 percent drop in the price of the bond. Similarly, if the duration of the bond is 10 years, a 1 percent increase in interest rates would lead to a 10 percent fall in the price of the bond. If rates drop by 1 percent, the price of the bond would be expected to go up by 10 percent.

The rule of thumb is based on this approximation formula:

$$PCP = -D_m \times \text{Change in yield}$$

where

PCP = Percentage change in bond price
D_m = Modified duration

The change in price due to duration (CP) is

$CP = - D_m \times$ Change in yield $\times$ Original price

New price = Original price + Change in price

Example. If modified duration is 2.53 years and the yield increases from 9 to 10 percent, the percentage change in the price of the bond (PCP) would be –2.53 percent, calculated as follows:

PCP	$= -2.53 \times (10\% - 9\%)$	$=$	-0.0253
CP	$= -2.53 \times (10\% - 9\%) \times 1000$	$=$	-25.30
New price	$= 1{,}000 - 25.30$	$=$	974.70

This rule of thumb is an approximation of the true percentage change in the price of the bond. This approximation can be improved by incorporating convexity in the formula. This is done later in this chapter.

Immunization. Immunization means sheltering a portfolio of bonds and mortgage-backed securities from the effects of interest rate changes. When a portfolio is immunized, interest rate changes do not affect the value of the portfolio.

A portfolio is immunized when the duration of the portfolio is set equal to the investor's investment horizon. For example, if an investor needs to save $20,000 by the end of a five-year period, she can buy a $20,000 zero-coupon Treasury bond that matures in five years. As long as the investor holds the bond for five years, she will receive $20,000 at maturity. The duration of the zero-coupon bond is five years and that is equal to the investor's investment horizon of five years.

With more complex portfolios, rebalancing may be required as time goes by so that the duration of the portfolio remains equal to the investment horizon.

CONVEXITY

Convexity also measures the responsiveness of bond prices to changes in interest rates or yields. When the effect of convexity is added to the effect of duration, one can get a better approximation of the percentage change in the bond price resulting from a 1 percent change in the yield of the bond.

Duration assumes that the price–yield relationship is linear but the actual relationship between the price of the bond and yield of the bond is a curve that is convex to the origin. Given the convexity of the price–yield curve, the change in the price of the bond due to duration resulting from a 1 percent increase in the yield overstates the drop in the price of the bond. In other words, it understates the new price. When the yield drops by 1 percent, the change in price due to duration understates the increase in price or understates the new price. For small changes in the yield, the errors are small, but for relatively big changes in yields, the errors are substantial.

Calculation of convexity. The calculation of convexity is also cumbersome, especially for long-term bonds, unless a computer program is used.

Example. Consider the following bond data:

Face amount	=	$1,000
Annual coupon rate	=	9%
Term in years	=	3
Yield to maturity	=	9%

The convexity is 9.02. See Table 18–2.

Convexity = $[1/(1+0.09)^2](1/1000)(10719.8) = 9.02$

The change in price due to convexity (CPC) is determined using the following formula:

$CPC = 0.5 \times$ Convexity $\times$ (Change in yield)$^2 \times$ Original price

$CPC = 0.5 \times 9.02 \times (0.01)^2 \times 1,000 = 0.45$

The combined effect of duration and convexity would be the sum of the two separate effects. For the preceding example, the combined effect is

Change in price due to duration	=	–25.30
Change in price due to convexity	=	0.45
Change in price due to duration and convexity	=	–24.85
New price = 1,000 – 24.85	=	975.15

TABLE 18–2
Calculation of Convexity

(1) Year (t)	(2) Cash Flow	(3) DF @ 9%	(4)=(2)×(3) PV(CF)	(5)=(1)+1 (t + 1)	(6)=(1)×(5)×(4) t × (t + 1) × (4)
1	90	0.9174	82.57	2	165.14
2	90	0.8417	75.75	3	454.51
3	1,090	0.7722	841.68	4	10,100.16
		Price =	1,000.00		10,719.80

DF =Discount factor
PV(CF) = Present values of cash flows

The combined effect gives a more accurate estimate of the change in the bond price. For small changes in the yield and for shorter-term bonds, the error of using just duration is minor. However, the bigger the change in yield, the lower the coupon payment and the longer the term to maturity, the greater the error will be and the greater the need to add the effect of convexity to the price change due to duration.

SUGGESTED READINGS

Bartlett, W. W. *The Valuation of Mortgage-Backed Securities*. Burr Ridge, IL: Richard D. Irwin, 1994.

Bierwag, G. O. *Duration Analysis*. Cambridge, MA: Ballinger Publishing, 1987.

Brooks, R., and M. Livingstone. "Relative Impact of Duration and Convexity on Bond Price Changes." *Financial Practice & Education*, Spring/Summer 1992, pp. 93–99.

Fabozzi, F. J. *Fixed Income Mathematics*. Burr Ridge, IL: Irwin Professional Publishing, 1993.

Fabozzi, F. J., and T. D. Fabozzi. *Handbook of Fixed-Income Securities*. Burr Ridge, IL: Richard D. Irwin, 1995.

_____. *Bond Markets, Analysis & Strategies*. Englewood Cliffs, NJ: Prentice Hall, 1989.

Fabozzi, F. J., and F. Modigliani. *Mortgage & Mortgage-Backed Securities Markets*. Boston: Harvard Business School Press, 1992.

Reilly, F. K. *Investment Analysis & Portfolio Management*. Ft. Worth, TX: Dryden Press, 1994.

Reilly, F. K., and R. S. Sidhu. "The Many Uses of Bond Duration." *Financial Analysts Journal*, July/August 1980, pp. 58–72.

Chapter Nineteen

Financial Ratios

As a previous chapter pointed out, investors use financial ratios to evaluate the profitability, liquidity, asset utilization, and debt position of a business entity. This chapter reviews measures of liquidity and debt utilization. In addition, we present a bankruptcy prediction model and ratios used in evaluating real estate loans.

LIQUIDITY RATIOS

A business firm needs liquid assets to meet its current liabilities. The adequacy of its liquid assets is measured by liquidity ratios. Two widely used measures of liquidity are the current ratio and the quick ratio, or acid test ratio.

Current Ratio

The current ratio is the ratio of current assets to current liabilities. If it is less than one, current assets are less than current liabilities and the business may not be able to pay off current liabilities. If it is greater than one, its current assets exceed its current liabilities.

The current ratio should be greater than one. It should exceed one by a comfortable margin. What is a comfortable margin depends on the industry in which the firm is located. In some industries, the average current ratio may be 1.5; in others, it may be 2, and so on. For a meaningful interpretation, the current ratio of a firm has to be compared to the industry average.

Quick Ratio

Some current assets are less liquid than others. They may be difficult to sell quickly and with little or no loss. For this reason, another measure of liquidity—the quick ratio—is used. The quick ratio, also called the *acid test ratio*, is calculated as follows:

$$QR = QA / CL$$

where

QR = Quick ratio
QA = Quick assets = Current assets – Inventory
CL = Current liabilities

The quick ratio also should be greater than one; however, for proper interpretation, it should be compared to the industry average.

DEBT UTILIZATION RATIOS

There are benefits to using debt. First, it provides leverage. Debt allows the firm to purchase assets that it could not purchase with just equity. The firm's equity may not be large enough to finance the desired amount of assets. If the business is profitable, the debt also can increase the rate of return on equity. Second, debt generates tax benefits. The interest on the debt is tax-deductible.

However, debt also can work against the firm. Interest on the debt has to be paid regularly whether the firm makes profits or not. The interest payments can be quite a burden if the firm has a considerable amount of debt and the net income of the firm is volatile. Also, when the business sustains losses, leverage lowers the rate of return on equity.

Debt ratios are used to analyze the debt position of a firm. The ratios help in determining whether the firm has excessive debt or not. Five debt ratios are presented here. They are the total assets to total liabilities ratio, the long-term debt to equity ratio, interest coverage, margin of safety, and the fixed charges coverage.

Total Assets to Total Liabilities Ratio

The total assets to total liabilities ratio is self-explanatory. It shows the extent to which total assets are financed by total liabilities. It measures financial leverage.

Long-Term Debt to Equity Ratio

The long-term debt to equity ratio is also self-explanatory. It shows the capitalization of the firm; that is, the composition of the long-term sources of funds for the business.

Interest Coverage

The interest coverage, also called *times interest earned*, is the ratio of earnings before interest and taxes (EBIT) to interest expense. If it is one, it means the firm has just enough earnings to cover interest expense. It could not afford to have a drop in its EBIT. EBIT should exceed interest expense by a comfortable margin. For example, if EBIT is 100 and interest expense is 20, the interest coverage is 5, calculated as follows:

Interest coverage $= EBIT/I = 100/20 = 5$

Margin of Safety

A formula related to the interest coverage is the margin of safety. It shows the extent to which EBIT has to fall before the firm becomes unable to pay interest out of earnings. If the interest coverage is one, the margin of safety becomes zero.

For the example in the previous paragraph, the margin of safety is 80 percent, calculated as follows:

$$MS = 1 - (1/IC) = 1 - (1/5) = 0.80, \text{ or } 80\%$$

where

IC = Interest coverage
MS = Margin of safety

Since the EBIT is five times bigger than the interest expense, EBIT could fall by 80 percent and the firm would still be able to cover its interest expense.

Fixed Charges Coverage

In addition to interest payments, the company may have other fixed payment obligations such as lease payments, preferred dividends, and sinking fund payments. The first two payments are tax-deductible but the last two are not. They are paid with after-tax profits. For this reason, they have to be expressed on a before-tax basis by dividing each one of them by (1 – Marginal tax rate of the firm). The formula for the fixed charges coverage is

$$FCC = \frac{EBIT + LP}{I + LP + \dfrac{(PD + SFP)}{(1 - t)}}$$

where

FCC = Fixed charges coverage
$EBIT$ = Earnings before interest and taxes
LP = Lease payments
I = Interest expense
PD = Preferred dividends
SFP = Sinking fund payments
t = Marginal tax rate

Example. Consider the following data:

Earnings before interest and taxes	=	100
Lease payments	=	5
Interest expense	=	10
Preferred dividends	=	2
Sinking fund payments	=	3
Marginal tax rate	=	34%

$$FCC = \frac{100 + 5}{10 + 5 + \dfrac{(2 + 3)}{(1 - 0.34)}} = 4.65$$

BANKRUPTCY PREDICTION MODELS

A number of studies have been made to see if a combination of financial ratios could predict bankruptcy. Since the number of financial ratios is large and the ratios useful for predicting bankruptcies are not known in advance, a statistical method called *discriminant analysis* is used not only to identify the ratios that are statistically significant in predicting bankruptcy but also to determine the weights for combining them into a weighted score. The score is then used to discriminate between firms that are bankrupt and those that are not.

The most widely known bankruptcy prediction model is probably the one developed by Altman. It is called Altman's Z score.

The formula for Altman's Z score is

$$Z = 1.2(X1) + 1.4(X2) + 3.3(X3) + 0.6(X4) + 1.0(X5)$$

where

$X1$ = Working capital/Total assets
$X2$ = Retained earnings/Total assets
$X3$ = Earnings before interest and taxes/Total assets
$X4$ = Market value of equity/Book value of total debt
$X5$ = Net sales/Total assets

If $Z > 3$, a company is presumed to be safe. If $Z < 1.81$, it is bankrupt. There is a gray area or zone of ignorance when Z is between 1.81 and 3. It is difficult to classify a firm whose Z score falls in that range.

Since the model requires the market value of equity, it is not appropriate for closely held or nonpublic companies. However, if an analyst still wants to use it, the market value of equity could be replaced by the book value of equity but the result would probably be less reliable.

Comprehensive example. The balance sheet and income statement of Alpha, Inc., are shown in Table 19–1 and Table 19–2 respectively. The two statements are used to calculate the various ratios just presented and the Z score.

TABLE 19–1
Balance Sheet of Alpha, Inc. ($ in millions)

	December 31,	
	1996	*1995*
Assets		
Cash and equivalents	$ 20	$ 20
Accounts receivable	150	145
Inventory	100	90
Other current assets	5	5
Total current assets	275	260
Property, plant, and equipment less accumulated depreciation	470	460
Total assets	$745	$720
Liabilities		
Accounts payable	$100	$ 90
Wages payable	22	23
Taxes payable	23	20
Other current liabilities	5	2
Total current liabilities	150	135
Long-term liabilities	250	250
Total liabilities	$400	$385
Stockholders' Equity		
Common stock (100 shares)	$100	$100
Retained earnings	245	235
Total stockholders' equity	345	335
Total liabilities and equity	$745	$720
Market value of equity	$300	

TABLE 19–2
Income Statement of Alpha, Inc.

	December 31,	
For the year ended:	1996	1995
Gross sales	$1,000	$800
− returns and discounts	5	4
= Net sales	995	796
− Cost of goods sold	500	396
= Gross profit or margin	495	400
− Operating expenses	295	210
= Operating income or profit	200	190
− Interest	10	5
= Earnings before taxes	190	185
− Income taxes	40	37
= Net income	150	148
− Dividends	50	50
= Retained earnings	$ 100	$ 98

Calculated financial ratios for Alpha, Inc.

Current ratio = 275/150 = 1.83
Quick ratio = 175/150 = 1.17
Total assets to total liabilities ratio = 745/400 = 1.86
Long-term debt to equity ratio = 250/345 = 0.72
Interest coverage = 200/10 = 20
Margin of safety = 1 − (1/20) = 0.95
Fixed charges coverage = 200/10 = 20

Altman's Z score =

$$Z = 1.2[(275 - 150)/745] + 1.4(100/745) + 3.3(200/745) + 0.6(300/400) + 1.0(995/745)$$

$$= 3.07$$

Since Z > 3, Alpha, Inc., is presumed to be safe.

RATIOS USED IN ANALYZING
COMMERCIAL REAL ESTATE LOANS

Several ratios are used for evaluating the risks associated with commercial real estate loans. We present three ratios—the debt coverage ratio, the operating expense ratio, and the break-even ratio.

Debt Coverage Ratio

The debt coverage ratio is the ratio of the property's net operating income to the annual debt service (principal and interest payments). It measures the ability of the real estate project to cover the annual debt payments. Lenders specify a minimum debt coverage ratio such as 1.2 for approving a loan. The smaller the ratio, the riskier the project is.

Operating Expense Ratio

The operating expense ratio is the ratio of operating expenses to effective gross income. The higher this ratio is, the riskier the project. Lenders may specify a maximum operating expense ratio such as 80 percent.

Break-even Ratio

The operating expense ratio does not take into account debt service. The break-even ratio does. It is calculated as follows:

$$BR = (OE + DS)/EGI$$

where

BR = Break-even ratio
OE = Operating expenses
DS = Debt service
EGI = Effective gross income

The lower the break-even ratio the better. The closer it is to one, the greater the risk associated with the project.

Example. Consider the following data:

Potential gross income	=	$2,500,000
– Vacancy costs	=	125,000
= Effective gross income	=	2,375,000
– Operating expenses	=	1,000,000
= Net operating income	=	1,375,000
– Debt service	=	822,217
= Cash flow before taxes	=	552,783

The ratios corresponding to these data are

Debt coverage ratio	= 1,375,000/822,217	= 1.67
Operating expense ratio	= 1,000,000/2,375,000	= 0.42
Break-even ratio	= 1,822,217/2,375,000	= 0.77

These ratios are useful in assessing the risk of a real estate project but they are by no means the only ratios used for analyzing a project. Other ratios used are the loan to value ratio, rent per square foot, operating expenses per square foot, and cost of land to net rentable area ratio. The financial condition and the track record of the developer are also very important.

SUGGESTED READINGS

Brueggeman, W. B., and J. D. Fisher. *Real Estate Finance & Investments*. Burr Ridge, IL: Richard D. Irwin, 1993.

Frase, L. M. *Understanding Financial Statements*. Englewood Cliffs, NJ: Prentice Hall, 1995.

Fridson, M. S. *Financial Statement Analysis*. New York: John Wiley & Sons, 1995.

Gibson, C. H. *Financial Statement Analysis*. Boston: PWS-Kent Publishing, 1989.

Gordon, G. *Understanding Financial Statements*. Cincinnati, OH: South-Western Publishing, 1992.

Hirt, G. A., and S. B. Block. *Fundamentals of Investment Management*. Burr Ridge, IL: Richard D. Irwin, 1993.

Maness, T. S., and J. W. Henderson. *Financial Analysis & Forecasting*. Engle-wood Cliffs, NJ: Prentice Hall, 1991.

Shenkel, W. M. *Real Estate Finance & Analysis*. Plano, TX: Business Publica-tions, 1988.

Weston, J. F., and T. E. Copeland. *Managerial Finance*. Ft. Worth, TX: Dryden Press, 1992.

Index